W9-ARB-934

# Women, Food and God

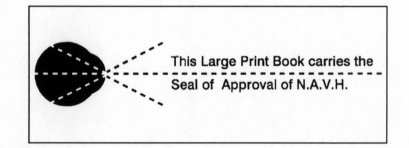

This Large Print Book carries the
Seal of Approval of N.A.V.H.

# WOMEN, FOOD AND GOD

## AN UNEXPECTED PATH
## TO ALMOST EVERYTHING

## GENEEN ROTH

**WHEELER PUBLISHING**
*A part of Gale, Cengage Learning*

GALE
CENGAGE Learning™

Detroit • New York • San Francisco • New Haven, Conn • Waterville, Maine • London

**GALE**
CENGAGE Learning™

Copyright © 2010 by Geneen Roth & Associates, Inc.
Wheeler Publishing, a part of Gale, Cengage Learning.

**LIBRARY OF CONGRESS CATALOGING-IN-PUBLICATION DATA**

Roth, Geneen.
  Women, food and God : an unexpected path to almost
everything / by Geneen Roth. — Large print ed.
    p. cm.
  Originally published: New York : Scribner, c2010.
  ISBN-13: 978-1-4104-3011-3 (hardcover)
  ISBN-10: 1-4104-3011-1 (hardcover)
  1. Compulsive eating—Psychological aspects. 2. Food
habits—Psychological aspects. 3. Obesity—Psychological
aspects. 4. Self-help techniques. I. Title.
RC552.C65R674 2010
616.85'26—dc22                                    2010019506

Published in 2010 by arrangement with Scribner, a division of Simon &
Schuster, Inc.

Printed in the United States of America
1 2 3 4 5 6 7 14 13 12 11 10

*For those who despair that there is no way through.*
*And for my retreat students,*
*who are living testimony that there is.*
*This is for you.*

# CONTENTS

8

# PROLOGUE:
## THE WORLD ON OUR PLATES

Eighty hungry women are sitting in a circle with bowls of cold tomato vegetable soup; they are glowering at me, furious. It is lunchtime on the third day of the retreat. During these daily eating meditations each woman approaches the buffet table, lines up to be served, takes her seat in the circle, and waits until we all sit down to eat. The process is agonizingly slow — fifteen minutes or so — especially if food is your drug of choice.

Although the retreat is going well and many people here have had life-changing insights, at this moment no one cares. They don't care about stunning breakthroughs or having ninety pounds to lose or whether God exists. They want to be left alone with their food, period. They want me to take my fancy ideas about the link between spirituality and compulsive eating and go away. It is one thing to be conscious about food in the meditation hall, and another to be sitting in the dining room, refraining from taking even one bite until the entire group has been served. Also, I've asked that silence be observed, so there are no frissons of laughter or chatty how-are-yous to distract attention from hunger or lack of it, since not everyone is hungry.

The retreat is based on a philosophy I've developed over the past thirty years: that our relationship to food is an exact microcosm of our relationship to life itself. I believe we are walking, talking expressions of our deepest convictions; everything we believe about love, fear, transformation and God is revealed in how, when and what we eat. When we inhale Reese's peanut butter cups when we are not hungry, we are acting out an entire world of hope or hopelessness, of faith or doubt, of love or fear. If we are interested in finding out what we actually believe — not what we think, not what we say, but what our souls are convinced is the bottom-line truth about life and afterlife — we need go no further than the food on our plates. God is not just in the details; God is also in the muffins, the fried sweet potatoes and the tomato vegetable soup. God — however we define him or her — is on our plates.

Which is why eighty women and I are sitting in a circle with cold vegetable soup. I look around the room. Photographs of flowers — intricate close-ups of a red dahlia, the golden edges of a white rose — are hung on the wall. A bouquet of peach gladiolas is splayed so extravagantly on a side table that it looks as if it is prancing at the prom in its finery. Then I begin noticing the faces of my students. Marjorie, a psychologist in her fifties, is playing with her spoon and doesn't meet my eyes. A twenty-year-old gymnast named Patricia is wearing black tights and a lemon-colored tank top. Her tiny body sits like an origami bird on her cushion — delicate, perfectly erect. On her plate is a handful of sprouts and a fistful of salad, that's all. I look to my right and see Anna, a surgeon from Mexico City, biting one of her lips and tapping her fork on the plate impatiently. There are three pieces of bread with thick slabs of butter on her plate, a bit of salad, no soup, no vegetables. Her food says, "Fuck you, Geneen, I don't have to play this ridiculous game. Watch me binge the second I get the chance." I nod at her as if to say, "Yup, I understand how hard it is to slow down." I take a quick glance around the rest of the room, at faces, at plates. The air is thick with resistance to

11

this eating meditation, and since I am the one who makes the rules, I am also the one at whom the fury is directed. Getting between people and their food is like standing in front of a speeding train; the act of being stopped in compulsive behavior is not exactly met with good cheer.

"Anyone want to say anything before we begin?" I ask.

Silence.

"Then, blessings on our food and all that made it possible. The rain, the sun, the people who grew it, brought it here, served it here," I say.

I can hear Amanda, who is sitting to my right, taking a deep breath at the sound of the prayer. Across the room Zoe nods her head, as if to say, "Oh, right. The earth, the sun, the rain. Glad they're there." But not everyone is grateful to take one more second to do anything but eat. Louisa in her bright red running suit sighs and grunts an almost indiscernible "Oh for God's sakes. Can we puh-leese get on with this?!" She looks as if she is ready to kill me. Humanely, of course, and only with the slightest bit of suffering, but still.

"Now, take some time and notice what you put on your plate," I say. "Notice if you were hungry when you chose the food. If you weren't physically hungry, was there another kind of hunger present?

"And looking at your plates, decide what you want to eat first and take a few bites. Notice how the food feels in your mouth. If it tastes like you thought it would taste. If it does what you thought it would do."

Three, four minutes pass amid the symphony of eating sounds: rustling, chewing, swallowing, clinking. I notice that Izzy, a six-foot-two willowy woman from France, is looking out the window and seems to have forgotten that we are eating. But most people are holding the plates up to their mouths so they can get the bites in faster.

Laurie, a thirty-five-year-old CEO of a Boston mortgage company, raises her hand. "I am not hungry, but I want to be. I want to eat anyway."

"Why is that?" I ask.

"Because it looks good and it's here, right now. It's the best comfort in town. What's wrong with wanting comfort from food?"

"Not a thing," I say. "Food is good and comfort is good. Except that when you are not hungry and you want comfort, food is only a temporary palliative; why not address the discomfort directly?"

"It's too hard to address things directly, too painful, and there isn't any end to it.

And if it's going to be endlessly painful, then at least I have food," she answers.

"So you figure that the best you can get out of life is cold vegetable soup?"

When she talks again, her voice is quivering. "It's the only true comfort I have, and I am not going to deprive myself of it." A tear jogs down her right cheek, hovers on her top lip. Heads nod in assent. A wave of murmurs passes around the circle.

Laurie says, "This thing we do here — waiting in silence until everyone gets their food — reminds me of what it was like to eat dinner in our family. My mother was drinking, my father was furious and no one was talking. It was horrible."

"What were you feeling during those times?" I ask.

"Lonely, miserable, like I was born into the wrong family. I wanted to escape but there was no place to go; I felt trapped. And this feels the same way. Like all of you are crazy and I am trapped here, with a bunch of loonies."

More head nods. More murmurs. A woman from Australia looks at me defiantly, her black waist-length hair brushing the edge of the soup bowl. I imagine she is thinking that Laurie is right and can she get a ride to the airport in fifteen minutes.

But right here, right now, in the center of this wound — *I've been abandoned and betrayed by who and what really matters and what I've got left is food* — is where the link between food and God exists. It marks the moment when we gave up on ourselves, on change, on life. It marks the place where we are afraid. It marks the feelings we won't allow ourselves to feel, and in so doing, keeps our lives constricted and dry and stale. In that isolated place, it is a short step to the conclusion that God — where goodness and healing and love exist — abandoned us, betrayed us or is a supernatural version of our parents. Our practice at the retreats of working through this despair is not one of exerting will or conjuring up faith, but being curious, gentle and engaged with the cynicism, the hopelessness, the anger.

I ask Laurie if she can make room for the part of her that feels trapped and lonely.

She says no, she can't. She says she just wants to eat.

I ask her if she is willing to consider the possibility that this has nothing to do with food.

She says no, she can't. She is staring at me with a look of grim determination that says, "Keep out. Go away. Not interested." Her eyes are narrow, her mouth is tight.

The room feels as if the air has been sucked out of it. People have stopped breathing; they are staring at me, at Laurie, waiting.

"I am wondering," I say, "why you are so intent on keeping me out. It seems as if there is a part of you bent on isolation, maybe even destruction."

She puts down her spoon, which she has been holding in midair, and stares at me.

"Have you given up?" I ask.

It's a risky question because it plunges right into the despair, but I ask it, since she has been fighting with me for the past three days and I am concerned about her leaving the retreat in a state of stony withdrawal. "When did the determination not to believe in anything ever again set in?"

She inhales sharply. Sits without speaking for a few minutes.

I look around the room. Suzanne, a mother of three young children, is crying. Victoria, a psychiatrist from Michigan, is watching, waiting, absorbed in what is happening.

"I've wanted to die since I was about ten," Laurie says quietly.

"Can you make room for the ten-year-old?" I ask. "The one who didn't see any way out of the hopeless situation she found herself in? Very gently, see if you can sense the hurt itself."

Laurie nods her head. "I think I can do that," she says quietly.

I ask her to do this not so that she can comfort her "inner child." I don't believe in inner children. I do believe that there are frozen places in ourselves — undigested pockets of pain — that need to be recognized and welcomed, so that we can contact that which has never been hurt or wounded or hungry. Although the work we do at the retreat is often experienced as therapeutic, it is not therapy. Unlike therapy, it is not designed to bolster self-esteem, which was created in reaction to our past. The work at the retreat is designed to reveal that which is beyond self-esteem, unconditioned by our past. Our personality and its defenses, one of which is our emotionally charged relationship to food, are a direct link to our spirituality. They are the bread crumbs leading us home.

Laurie says, "I don't know what just happened, but suddenly I have no desire to eat the soup."

I say, "It seems as if there is something even better than food: touching what you considered untouchable and viscerally discovering that you are bigger than your pain."

She nods her head and smiles for the first time in three days. "Life doesn't seem so bad at this moment. Saying out loud how bad I thought it was when I was ten makes it seem not so bad now. I guess what happens is that I can feel the ten-year-old and how big her sadness was without totally becoming her — that's a good thing."

The simple fact that her pain can be touched and that it won't destroy her means that all is not lost or hopeless or unredeemable. I nod my head and ask if she wants to keep talking to me. She says, "I think this is enough for now."

I ask people to pick up their silverware and take a few more bites — noticing what they want to eat, how it tastes, how they feel.

A few minutes later, Nell, a student at the retreats for seven years, raises her hand. "I am not hungry anymore, but I suddenly realized that I am afraid to push the food away."

"Why?" I ask.

"Because . . ." — and she starts to cry — ". . . because I realize I am not broken . . . and that you will be angry at me if you know."

"Why would I be angry at you?" I ask.

"Because you'd see who I really am and you wouldn't like it."

"What would I see?"

"Vitality. A lot of energy. Determination. Strength."

"Wow," I say. "And what wouldn't I like about that?"

"I wouldn't need you then. And you would be threatened by that."

"Who are you taking me to be? Anyone you know who was threatened by how gorgeous you are?"

Nell starts to laugh. "Hi, Mom," she says.

The room erupts in a wave of laughter.

"She was so depressed," Nell says. "And if I was just myself, that was too much for her. I needed to shut down the bigness — I needed to be as broken as she was — otherwise she'd reject me and that was unacceptable."

"What's happening in your body, Nell?" I ask.

"It feels like a fountain of color," she says. "It's as if I am streaming with vivid hues of red, green, gold, black streaking in my chest, my arms, my legs . . ."

"OK, let's stop here for a minute. . . ."

I look around the room. Anna, who'd wanted to tell me to fuck off, is crying. Camille, who has looked bored since the retreat started, seems utterly absorbed in what is happening. The group attention is riveted by what Nell is saying about the need to be broken. They can relate to the belief that if they keep themselves wounded and damaged, they will be loved.

I look at Nell and say, "When you stop and let yourself feel what is being offered to you, it is never, ever what you thought it would be. You go from being afraid to being a fountain in three minutes. . . ."

Nell says, "It feels as if this quiet, calm space has been waiting for me to come back to it, like it's been here all my life, like it's more me than anything else." And then Nell stands up and looks around the room. She pulls her chair aside and says, "Listen to this, girls! I AM NOT BROKEN!!!!"

More laughter. Then Nell continues, "This process amazes me. First I had to deal with the food thing. I really did have to stop using food to comfort myself — otherwise I felt too crazy — and there was no time for this spiritual stuff. Then, when my eating calmed down, I had to at least allow myself to feel the feelings of brokenness — that was tough. That was the part where I just had to believe what you were saying, Geneen — that my resistance to the pain was worse than the pain. But to actually feel that I am not broken — I can hardly explain what that is like. It's like being a piece of holiness. It's like saying that goodness is not just for everyone else, it's also for me. It *is* me!"

Since it's almost time for the next session to begin in the meditation hall, I ask people to check in with their hunger levels, to rate themselves on a scale of one to ten, with one being hungry and ten being full, and to eat accordingly. "We'll meet down in the meditation hall in thirty minutes," I say, standing up from my seat.

As I am about to walk out the door, a woman named Marie grabs my hand and says, "I just have to say one thing to the group. Is that OK?"

I nod my head, bracing myself for what is coming. Marie has been a skeptic since the retreat began. She has sat in the sessions glaring at me with her arms folded across her chest as if to say, "Prove it to me, honey. Prove that this food thing is anything more than just shutting my mouth." After each talk I've given, she's challenged me, confronted me; yesterday she told me she was sorry she ever came. "This is just AFGO," she said. "And I'm tired of it. I just want to lose the damn weight and be done with it."

"What's AFGO?" I asked.

"Another Fucking Growth Opportunity," Marie answered.

I laughed so hard I started snorting. "I'm sorry for laughing," I said. "But it seems as if AFGOs have gotten a bad rap. Maybe you will find that this retreat opens you in ways you never imagined."

"I doubt it," she answered, and stomped away, her loose ponytail of curly red hair bobbing as her body receded in the distance.

Now, in the dining room, Marie says, "It just occurred to me that everything we believe about our lives is right here. The whole world is on these plates."

"Amen, sister," I say. Before stepping out the door, I bend down to Marie's ear and quietly say, "Let's hear it for AFGOs."

On my way to the meditation hall, I am once again aware that the entire retreat could take place in the dining room, that what we believe about food and eating is an exquisite reflection of all our beliefs. As soon as the food comes out, the feelings come out. As soon as the feelings come out, there is an inevitable recognition of the self-inflicted violence and suffering that fuel any obsession. And on the heels of that recognition comes the willingness to engage with and unwind the suffering rather than be its prisoner. The exquisite paradox of this engagement is that when the suffering is fully allowed, it dissolves. Weight loss occurs easily, naturally. And without the self-inflicted pain and the stories about what is wrong, what's left is what was there before they began: our connection to meaning and to that which we find holy.

In 1978, I led my first group for compulsive eaters; at the initial meeting I was fifty pounds overweight and, due to a misunderstanding with a hairdresser friend who'd given me a permanent, was sporting a set of rollers in my hair.

Months earlier, a few hours away from killing myself after gaining eighty pounds in two months, I'd made the radical decision to stop dieting and eat what my body wanted. Since adolescence, I'd gained and lost over a thousand pounds. I'd been addicted to amphetamines for four years and to laxatives for two years. I'd thrown up, spit up, fasted and tried every diet possible, from the All-Grape-Nuts diet to the One-Hot-Fudge-Sundae-a-Day diet to Atkins, Stillman and Weight Watchers. I'd been anorexic — spending almost two years weighing eighty pounds — and I'd been quite overweight. Mostly overweight. My closet was stuffed with eight different sizes of pants, dresses and blouses. Crazed with self-loathing and shame, I vacillated between wanting to destroy myself and wanting to fix myself with the next best promise of losing thirty pounds in thirty days.

By that first dollar-a-session group, I'd been eating what my body wanted for a few months. I had lost a few pounds — a major accomplishment for someone who believed that she'd be living in diet hell until her last breath — and it was slowly dawning on me that my relationship with food had affected every other part of my life.

Those women who did not run screaming in the opposite direction when they realized that the overweight woman with rollers in her hair was — no kidding — the leader of the group met with me weekly for two years as we explored the role food was playing in our lives. Until my first book, *Feeding the Hungry Heart,* was published in 1982 and I began teaching all over the country — in Alaska, Minnesota, Florida, New York — I worked with hundreds more women in weekly groups. Women who swore that they'd always need to lock their food in their kitchen cabinets and hide the key were suddenly able to eat one of something — one bowl, one piece, one bite. Women who had never been able to lose weight were suddenly finding their clothes too baggy, their waistbands too loose.

Within a year after I stopped dieting, I'd reached my natural weight, where I've remained for three decades. But more than the new body size, it was the lightness of being that enthralled me; although I didn't quite understand the connection between trusting myself around food and trusting less tangible hungers (for rest, contact, meaning), the relationship with food became the lens through which I began to see almost everything.

Zen master Shunryu Suzuki Roshi said that enlightenment was following one thing all the way to the end, and I soon suspected that if I tracked the impulse to eat when I wasn't hungry to its core, I'd find every single thing I believed about loving, living, and dying right there, in that moment. Which — following the relationship with food to the end — pretty much describes how I've spent the last thirty-two years.

When I offered my first six-day retreat in May 1999, it was supposed to be a one-off event. I wanted to bring the twin passions of my life together: my work with eating and my years of meditation and spiritual inquiry.

I'd meditated since 1974, lived in ashrams and monasteries, and was an ongoing student of the Diamond Approach, a nondenominational teaching that uses psychology as a bridge to spirituality. I still cringed when I heard the word *God,* and the word *spiritual* evoked a vision of piety and austerity that did not match — this would be an understatement — my vast collection of nubby sweaters and honey-colored boots. I still had about a dozen moments of neurosis per day, but I also had more moments of contentment and freedom than I ever imagined possible for a formerly fat girl from Queens. I wanted everyone to know what I knew, have what I had.

Still. I was stunned at what happened.

It wasn't the stories about bingeing or dieting or fasting I'd heard; it wasn't the tales of abuse or trauma. I'd heard most of them before. No, what shocked me was that after years of working with compulsive eating, I'd been treating it as a psychological and physical problem, and although it was both of those, I suddenly saw that it was also a doorway into a blazing inner universe.

After the first retreat, the students wanted to come back; they wanted to do it again. They reminded me of the afternoon I saw a full eclipse of the sun in Antigua. My husband and I were standing in the ocean with dozens of other people, wearing dark plastic glasses so that our eyes wouldn't get burned by the sun. We watched as the moon completely covered the sun. And we stood speechless in enchanted darkness. As the light slowly returned, someone yelled to the moon, "Again. Do it again."

Since we had an advantage over the moon — we *could* do it again — we did. And we still are.

As I've taught the retreats, I've learned that each of us has a basic view of reality and God that we act out every day in our relationship with our families, our friends, our food. It doesn't matter whether we believe in one God, many gods or no god. Anyone who breathes and thinks and experiences has beliefs about God. And since mothering is our first preverbal template for an existence in which we feel welcomed or rejected, loved or abandoned, many of us have fused our relationship with our mothers with our concepts of God.

Whether we are aware of those early experiences or believe in preverbal templates does not alter the truth: our daily lives, from the mundane to the sublime, from our reactions to sitting in traffic to our responses to the death of someone we love, are expressions — outpicturings — of our deepest beliefs.

To discover what you really believe, pay attention to the way you act — and to what you do when things don't go the way you think they should. Pay attention to what you value. Pay attention to how and on what you spend your time. Your money. And pay attention to the way you eat.

You will quickly discover if you believe the world is a hostile place and that you need to be in control of the immediate universe for things to go smoothly. You will discover if you believe there is not enough to go around and that taking more than you need is necessary for survival. You will find out if you believe that being quiet is unbearable, and that being alone means being lonely. If feeling your feelings means being destroyed. If being vulnerable is for sissies or if opening to love is a big mistake. And you will discover how you use food to express each one of these core beliefs.

The retreats now take place twice a year, and many of those first students, having worked through their painful eating and lost weight, are still coming as a way — as they call it — to come home to themselves.

Introductions (or, in this case, prologues)

are supposed to tell you who the book is written for and why you should read it. I'm probably not the best person to address these questions because it seems to me that every single person has a shtick with food and therefore everyone should read this book. Everyone who eats, everyone who wants to know why they can't stop eating, everyone who wants to use what they most want to get rid of (their addictions, their uncomfortable feelings, their unquestioned beliefs about their own limitations) as a path to what they most want more of (unruffled peace, everyday holiness and ease of being in body, mind and heart) should read this book. Also, anyone who has ever wondered about the meaning of life and/or questioned or felt abandoned by God.

Did I just include all living beings?

Probably, but as I said, I'm not objective in these matters, having spent two-thirds of my life astonished at the power and implications of the relationship with food.

Here, now, is almost every single thing I know about using eating as a doorway to freedom from suffering, the demystification of weight loss, and the luminous presence that so many call God.

■ ■ ■ ■

# PART ONE:
# PRINCIPLES

■ ■ ■ ■

# CHAPTER ONE:
## ABOUT GOD

I turned to Hostess Sno Balls the same year I gave up on God.

I was eleven years old and had been praying nightly for thick hair and a boyfriend, but mostly for my parents to stop screaming at each other. After a year, nothing had changed.

I'd heard about God from two sources: *The Ten Commandments* starring Charlton Heston and my friend Janey Delahunty, who wrote letters to him during Social Studies class. After I saw what God did to those Egyptians, I was positive he could give my parents a lesson or two on family peace. And when Janey described a God who read her letters and answered her prayers, I began praying, too, but couldn't bring myself to write. Years later, in *Children's Letters to God,* a child wrote (this is a paraphrase): "Dear God, I love my family but I wonder if you tried out anyone else before you sent me to them."

I didn't like praying. I didn't like getting down on my knees and talking to the air; it felt too much like begging for love that I already knew I couldn't have. When my prayers weren't answered, I felt ashamed for believing I could be saved; I decided that God saw something in my cells that was unredeemable — and that I was on my own.

At eleven, I felt like a raw nerve, as if the fact that I took up space at the red Formica table was the reason for the hatred between my parents and their violence toward each other. They threw things, left the house, stayed away for hours or days. My mother looked like a blond Sophia Loren, my brother looked like he belonged on *Leave It to Beaver,* but I had a moon face, stringy hair and ankles as thick as piano stools. Even Robert Grady, who smelled like dirty socks, wouldn't pick me to dance with him at our sixth-grade party.

Enter food.

The sight of a Hostess Sno Ball turned the world into a riot of color. The fluffy, pristine mound of marshmallow sprinkled with coconut. The promise of the chocolate cake inside. And then, oh, then, the cloud of white icing. For the time it took to eat four or six Sno Balls, my hair was curly, my legs were as long as Madi Isaacs's and my parents gazed adoringly at each other during picnics at Lake George, where we ate egg salad sandwiches with the crusts cut off. I turned to food for the same reasons that people turned to God: it was my sigh of ecstasy, my transport to heaven, my concrete proof that relief from the pain of everyday life was possible.

Then it would be gone.

The cellophane packages would be empty, the bits of coconut stuck in my teeth, and I'd convince myself that the reason I didn't have parents who held hands at parades was because I was fat. And so I started dieting the same year I started bingeing. Dieting gave me a purpose. Bingeing gave me relief from the relentless attempt to be someone else.

For almost two decades, the suffering I felt about anything — my parents' marriage, my boyfriend Sheldon's death, my chubby moon face — was expressed in my relationship with food. Overeating was my way to punish and shame myself; each time I gained weight, each time I failed at a diet, I proved to myself that my deepest fear was true: I was pathetic and doomed and I didn't deserve to live. I could have expressed this despair through drugs or shoplifting or alcohol, but I chose chocolate instead.

Dieting was like praying. It was a plaintive cry to whoever was listening: *I know I am fat. I know I am ugly. I know I am undisciplined, but see how hard I try. See how violently I restrict myself, deprive myself, punish myself. Surely there must be a reward for those who know how horrible they are.*

And precisely because dieting and bingeing were the main ways I was expressing my despair, the consequences of not dieting or bingeing were staggering. Making the decision to stop dieting was like committing heresy, like breaking a vow that was never supposed to be broken. It was like saying, "You were wrong, God. You were wrong, Mom. I am worth saving." And somehow, by deciding that I was no longer going to collude with the belief in my own degradation, something I never would have called me showed up: the presence of loveliness, the awareness of kindness and the unmistakable knowledge that I belonged here.

I had no name for this kindness. I didn't believe in God or mystical experiences, but there was no denying that I was having the direct experience of a nameless something that was bigger than my mind, my childhood, my stories of what was wrong and right. The only way I can explain this even now is say that my suffering reached a critical mass of desperation: either I was going to kill myself or a completely different way of living was going to be revealed. And while I realize that in many cases human suffering does not lead to revelation, in my case, for some reason, it did.

After that initial opening, it took years of questioning my old beliefs, years of spiritual and scientific exploration to make my way to a broader understanding of the presence that most people call God, but it was the pain of my relationship with food that opened the door.

I don't believe in the God with long white hair and X-ray vision that favors some people, some countries, some religions and not others. I don't believe in the sky dweller, the knower of all things, the granter of prayers. But I do believe in the world beyond appearances and that there is so much we can't see or touch or know just by looking. And I do believe — because I have experienced it again and again — that the world beyond appearances is as real as a chair, a dog, a teapot.

And I believe in love. And beauty. I believe that every single person has something they find beautiful and that they truly love. The smell of their child's hair, the silence of a forest, their lover's crooked grin. Their country, their religion, their family. And I believe that if you follow this love all the way to its end, if you start with the thing you find most beautiful and trace its perfume back to its essence, you will perceive an intangible presence, a swath of stillness that allows the thing you love to be visible like the openness of the sky reveals the presence of the moon.

I don't believe in the God that most people call God, but I do know that the only definition of God that makes any sense is one that uses this human life and its suffering — the very things we believe we need to hide or fix — as a path to the heart of love itself. Which is why the relationship with food is a perfect doorway.

While I realize that some people find the word *God* explosive and potentially divisive, and that others have a deeply satisfying relationship with God, I use the word in this book because it evokes a vast expanse that we cannot penetrate with our minds, although we *can* know it through silence or poetry or simply sensing what is always here.

And because pairing food with God fizzles the mind — the two seem as unrelated as titanium computers and scarlet peonies — all that you believe about food and God can fall away. And in the space of not knowing that remains, perhaps you will discover what I have experienced directly: that understanding the relationship with food is a direct path to coming home after a lifetime of being exiled. Perhaps that home is what God was always meant to be.

# CHAPTER TWO:
## ENDING THE WAR

On the first morning of my retreats, I tell my students that the great blessing of their lives is their relationship with food. They look at me rather quizzically, but the sentiment sounds so lovely that they are willing to hear me out. Then I say that we are not going to fix their relationship with food; we are actually going to walk through the door of their eating problem and see what's behind it. Instead of using food to avoid discomfort, they are going to learn how to tolerate what they believe is intolerable.

They stare. They scowl. They whisper to one another.

Why would any sane person believe that tolerating the intolerable is a worthy endeavor?

Mayhem is five minutes away.

Then, because it seems like the thing to do, I tell them the struggling, suffering, hellish part of my story. Over the last few decades I've discovered that stories of personal hell, sprinkled at tense and hostile moments, go a long way to diffusing bitterness. I describe the years of gaining and losing a thousand pounds, loathing myself, being suicidal. Then I talk about the switch to not dieting and eating what I wanted to eat.

I've told this story for many more years than I lived it, but it only recently became clear to me that the radical part of the tale is not that I stopped dieting; it's that I stopped trying to fix myself. I stopped fighting with myself, stopped blaming myself, my mother, my latest boyfriend for my weight. And since diets were my most flagrant attempts at fixing myself, I stopped them as well. I didn't care anymore that I was so fat that I could only fit into one summer dress in the middle of November; I had reached my threshold of struggling and figured I had two choices: stop dieting or kill myself.

Most of my students can't imagine a world in which they would stop dieting or trying to fix the size of their thighs. It is easier to imagine people coming back from the dead or Brad Pitt asking them to get married than to imagine themselves dropping the war with their bodies. They have whole friendships built on commiserating about the twenty pounds they have to lose and the jeans that are too tight and the latest greatest diets. They fit in by hating themselves. By trying hard and then harder to lose that last twenty, fifty, eighty pounds — and never being able to do it. The never being able to do it is necessary if they want to fit in. The constant war with food and body size is important if they want to be loved. They are like Sisyphus pushing the boulder up the mountain and almost getting there but never actually arriving.

The great thing about being Sisyphus is that you have your work cut out for you. You always have something to do. As long as you are striving and pushing and trying hard to do something that can never be done, you know who you are: someone with a weight problem who is working hard to be thin. You don't have to feel lost or helpless because you always have a goal and that goal can never be reached.

In an April 2007 UCLA study of the effectiveness of dieting, researchers found that one of the best predictors of weight gain was having lost weight on a diet at some point during the years before the study started. Among those who were followed for fewer than two years, 83 percent gained back more weight than they had lost. Another study found that people who went on diets were *worse* off than people who didn't.

Failing is built into the weight game. There is no way to play it and win.

I read these studies to my retreat students. I say, "If you were ill and the doctor suggested a cure that would make you WORSE, would you follow it nonetheless?" I expect them to say, "Of course not." I expect them to realize they have been brainwashed by a sixty-billion-dollar-a-year diet industry.

Instead, at least one person says, "You lost me when you got to the part about the summer dress in mid-November." Someone else nods. The general feeling in the room is that they'd rather be blind or paralyzed than wear a summer dress with an elastic waistband in the middle of November. If a full-scale war with themselves is what it takes to avoid being fat, if they need to keep blaming themselves and their mothers and their partners for their relationship with food, if their self-worth is increasingly shredded with every failure to stay on their diets, well, so what. Every war has collateral damage.

During the first few days of a retreat, people are convinced that I have the answer to the puzzles of their lives. They really truly believe that there is something that will fix their weight problems and thereby fix what they can't put into words: what it feels like to be them. To live their particular lives, with their particular families, with their particular minds. What it's like to have insulin-dependent diabetes or a friend who was just diagnosed with breast cancer. They realize intellectually that losing weight will not take their friend's cancer away, but the promise of weight loss is that it will allow them to live on a magical piece of earth from which everything else will be manageable.

One woman told me that it wasn't weight loss she wanted but to feel lean and trim, as if she wasn't carrying any excess baggage. Then she said that, oh, by the way, the love of her life had died a few years ago, and that the next man she got involved with died three weeks ago of a heart attack. "But what I need most of all," she said, "is to be trim and lean, I need that. I really need that."

When I asked her how she felt about losing two people she loved within a few years, she answered matter-of-factly, "I always get deserted. I always get abandoned."

"Always?" I asked.

"Yes," she said, "always."

When I questioned her about the "always" belief, when I asked about her feelings of abandonment, she said, "I can't feel those feelings. They will wipe me away, tear me apart. What I need to focus on is being lean and trim. Then I will be able to cope with all of it."

In her mind, being lean meant being strong enough to deal with the messy feelings she didn't want to feel. With heartbreak, with loss. With being alone.

*If my body is in shape — which it never has been and probably never will be — then I will be able to feel what I can't feel now.*

*If I fix myself so that I am no longer myself, then everything will be fine. My feelings will be manageable.*

A student of mine said, "If I stop trying to be thin, I'd either eat so much that I'd take up two seats on the plane or else I'd be so lost that I'd become a bag lady who sleeps on church steps."

And while I have no doubt that using the relationship with food as a microcosm of our feelings about being alive actually leads to weight loss — I've seen it thousands of times — most people are still reluctant to end dieting and give up the war.

From Courtney E. Martin in *The Christian Scientist Monitor:* "So many perfect girls were raised entirely without organized religion, and the majority of the rest of us experienced 'spirituality' only in the form of mandatory holiday services with a big-haired grandmother. . . . Overlay our dearth of spiritual exploration with our excess of training in ambition . . . and you have a generation of godless girls . . . raised largely without a fundamental sense of divinity. In fact, our worth in the world has always been tied to our looks . . . not the amazing miracle of mere existence."

Women turn to food when they are not hungry because they *are* hungry for something they can't name: a connection to what is beyond the concerns of daily life. Something deathless, something sacred. But replacing the hunger for divine connection with Double Stuf Oreos is like giving a glass of sand to a person dying of thirst. It creates more thirst, more panic. Combine the utter inefficacy of dieting with the lack of spiritual awareness and we have generations of mad, ravenous, self-loathing women. We have become so obsessed with getting rid of our obsession, with riding on top of our suffering and ignoring its inherent message, that we lose the pieces of ourselves waiting to be found beneath it. But fixing ourselves is not the same as being ourselves. The real richness of obsession lies in the ineffable stillness, the irrefutable wholeness, that is found in turning toward its source.

Like everyone else in this diet-mad culture in which we live, my retreat students are loath to stop the frantic attempts to change themselves. They know that something is not quite right in their lives, and because they are not at their ideal weights, they believe that food is the problem and that dieting will fix it. When I suggest that they're trying to fix something that has never been broken, a wave of anxiety courses through the room.

They ask, "How could you say that nothing is broken when I can't fit into any of my clothes? When my husband won't touch me because I am too fat? When I am out of breath as I walk up the stairs? Can't you see that something is terribly terribly wrong?"

And I say, "Yes, something is wrong, but it will not be fixed through losing weight." (Since most of them have already been thin at least once, twice or dozens of times, they already know this but keep forgetting it.) "The relentless attempts to be thin take you further and further away from what could actually end your suffering: getting back in touch with who you really are. Your true nature. Your essence."

Arms are crossed, jaws are set. Ethereal anythings — essence, true nature, to the extent that they exist — can wait until they get thin.

I say, "Can you remember a time, perhaps when you were very young, when life as it was — just the fact that it was early morning or any old day in summer — was enough? When you were enough — not because of what you looked like or what you did, but just because everything was the way it was. Nothing was wrong. When you were sad, you cried and then it was over. You were back to a fundamental feeling of positivity, of goodness just because you were alive. What if you could live that way now? And what if your relationship to food was the doorway?"

In *The English Patient,* Michael Ondaatje writes: "A man in a desert can hold absence in his cupped hands knowing it is something that feeds him more than water. There is a plant [in the desert] whose heart, if one cuts it out, is replaced with a fluid containing herbal goodness. Every morning one can drink the liquid the amount of a missing heart."

Compulsive eating is an attempt to avoid

the absence (of love, comfort, knowing what to do) when we find ourselves in the desert of a particular moment, feeling, situation. In the process of resisting the emptiness, in the act of turning away from our feelings, of trying and trying again to lose the same twenty, fifty, eighty pounds, we ignore what could utterly transform us. But when we welcome what we most want to avoid, we evoke that in us that is not a story, not caught in the past, not some old image of ourselves. We evoke divinity itself. And in doing so, we can hold emptiness, old hurts, fear in our cupped hands and behold our missing hearts.

# Chapter Three: Never Underestimate the Inclination to Bolt

In the spring of 1982, I found myself on a pay phone trying frantically to rent a helicopter so I could leave the ten-day silent Buddhist retreat where I'd been for exactly fifteen hours. I'd returned from India a few years before and was searching for a spiritual path that did not include a frizzy-haired betel-sucking man who called himself the incarnation of God. My therapist, Kate, had urged me to sign up for the retreat, but she forgot to mention that I'd have to spend fifteen hours a day meditating — and I'd forgotten to ask. Kate also neglected to tell me that I couldn't talk or make eye contact with anyone the entire time.

The guy on the phone asked me where I was.

"In the middle of the desert," I answered. "Joshua Tree National Park."

"There are no helicopter pads there, lady, and even if there were, you're talking a lot of money. Thousands of dollars."

It was the second day of the retreat and I felt as if I was insane. In the shockingly silent meditation hall the night before, I had images of standing up and yelling, "Douche bag, douche bag!" like someone with Tourette's syndrome. Clearly I needed to leave.

I tried to think of alternatives to renting a helicopter — hitchhiking, begging, walking. None were feasible. Of the hundred and fifty people at the retreat — who I was now convinced were a cult of Buddhist zombies walking in slow meditative stupor around the grounds — I knew no one. My dorm room — with fifteen women and one bathroom — was crowded and stuffy, and despite the precept of nonviolence, I was ready to inflict great harm upon the snorer whose cot was next to mine. Bang her over the head with a large cactus.

Spending ten days stuck in my own mind felt like being locked up in a cramped cell with a crazy person and not having any way out.

"Twenty-five hundred dollars," the helicopter rental guy muttered, and since my salary as an avocado and cheese sandwich maker at a local health food store in Santa Cruz was six hundred dollars a month, flying out of the retreat was out of the question.

Buddhist teacher Pema Chodron writes, "Never underestimate the inclination to bolt."

I tell that to my students on the first night of the retreats. They laugh, they think, Me? I won't bolt. This thing with food has got me so down that I will do anything — *anything* — to resolve it.

On the first night they are too tired from having traveled across the country or an ocean or two. But by the second day they are making plans to fly home. Or they decide they are bored and there is no new information here. Often they decide using food isn't so bad after all and wonder if they can get their money back and leave for a cruise instead.

I tell them the helicopter story. I tell them that if compulsive eating is anything, it's a way we leave ourselves when life gets hard. When we don't want to notice what is going on. Compulsive eating is a way we distance ourselves from the way things are when they are not how we want them to be. I tell them that ending the obsession with food is all about the capacity to stay in the present moment. To not leave themselves. I tell them that they don't have to make a choice between losing weight and doing this. Weight loss is the easy part; anytime you truly listen to your hunger and fullness, you lose weight. But I also tell them that compulsive eating is basically a refusal to be fully alive. No matter what we weigh, those of us who are compulsive eaters have anorexia of the soul. We refuse to take in what sustains us. We live lives of deprivation. And when we can't stand it any longer, we binge. The way we are able to accomplish all of this is by the simple act of bolting — of leaving ourselves — hundreds of times a day.

But that doesn't touch the sudden realization — and the subsequent panic — that they really don't want to sit in the center of their own lives. It's one thing to say you want to stop using food to numb yourself. To be miserable about the size of your body. To feel as if you are killing yourself with double cheeseburgers and fries. But slowing down, asking yourself what is actually going on when you want to eat when you aren't hungry, watching how you inhale three muffins before you even realize you're eating — that's going too far. There is something about accepting the unpredictable fragility of this life that is just too much. So the very minute they begin feeling or sensing or thinking something that is uncomfortable, they want to get out of Dodge.

There are many ways to bolt. Walking out the door. Renting a helicopter. Distracting yourself from your pain by doing a thousand different things: thinking about something else, blaming your mother, blaming someone else, getting into a fight, comparing yourself to other people, dreaming about life in the future, recalling life in the past, never getting deeply involved.

Eating.

Spending your life trying to lose weight or figure it all out.

Resigning yourself to the endless struggle with food so you never have to take the dive into the meaning of it all. Or discover who you are, what your relationships can be without the drama of food.

Staying where you are with what you are feeling or seeing or sensing is the first step in ending the obsession with food. And although it seems as if ending the obsession is what we all want to do, we actually want to keep it more. And for very good reasons.

Obsession gives you something to do besides having your heart shattered by heart-shattering events. Like watching your children get sick, like living while your spouse dies. Like being with your parents as they get old, wear diapers, forget their own names. Obsession gives you a plane ticket out of a particular kind of heartbreak. It gives you a helicopter ride out of the desert. It creates a parallel world, a hologram of emotions, passions, breathtaking reversals. It gives you the illusion of feeling everything without having to be vulnerable to anything. In the drama of obsession, you are the star, the costar, the director, the producer. Other people, even your children, are only stand-ins. Cardboard props. When you are crazed about a binge, for example, you become so focused on getting the food in your mouth that you leave your child in the car, as one of my students did, and forget she's there. There is madness in obsession, yes, but its value is that it drowns out the madness of life. Especially now, when we are living on the verge of destroying ourselves and our environment. Not bolting — being awake without being drugged by food, alcohol, work, sex, money, drugs, fame or in denial (about the crisis we are actually in) — is asking a lot.

I used to think (well, okay, sometimes I still do) that the less I showed up, the less it would hurt when I lost everything. When

55

people I loved died. When things fell apart. Sometimes I shock myself. Sometimes I wish my husband, Matt, would just die and get it over with. In my most regressed moments (seeing events through the eyes of a child), I live between fearing doom and wishing for it, between worrying that Matt will die every time he walks out the door and convincing myself that I will be relieved when he does.

This is the very thinking that evolved into the obsession with food thirty years ago. The belief, unconscious as it was, that I couldn't handle, couldn't tolerate, didn't have thick enough skin or a resilient enough heart to withstand what was in front of me without fragmenting. Which is another way of saying that obsession is a way of organizing our lives so that we never have to deal with the hard part — the part that happens between being two years old and dying. While I realize that it's not all hard and that some people — Matt and perhaps one or two more — don't see it this way, we compulsive eaters wouldn't have an obsession with food if we believed that life was tolerable without it.

The glitch here is that it's not life in the present moment that is intolerable; the pain we are avoiding has already happened. We are living in reverse.

It's not that there isn't pain in the present moment. Every day I get letters from people about just making it through another day. This morning I got a letter from one of my students who told me that her mother got her hair done on Thursday like she always did and by Friday she was completely delusional and needed to be checked into a mental health facility. She said, "My father is torn apart. They've been married for sixty years. And I have no idea how I am going to get through this."

The answer to "I have no idea how I am going to get through this" is: You allow yourself to sob, to heave, to feel as if your heart has a boulder crashing through it. You sit with your father. You listen to his sorrow. You get help from your friends. And you notice that at the end of every day you are still alive. And you notice that when you don't use food to shut yourself down, to leave your body, you actually feel more alive. That feeling anything, even grief, is different from what you thought it would be. That when you don't leave yourself, a different life is lived. One that includes vulnerability and tenderness and fragility and changes the landscape — makes it verdant, wider, breathtaking — of life as you know it.

To the extent that we go into survival mode — I can't feel this, I won't feel this, it hurts too much, it will kill me — we are slipping into baby skins, old forms, familiar selves. Young children, especially infants, mediate the pain of loss or abandonment or abuse through the body; there is no difference between physical and emotional pain. If the pain is too intense and the defenses are too weak, a child will become psychotic and/or die. It is lifesaving for a child to develop defenses that allow her to leave a situation she can't physically leave by shutting down her feelings or turning to something that soothes her. But if as adults we still believe that pain will kill us, we are seeing through the eyes of the fragile selves we once were and relying on the exquisite defense we once developed: bolting. Obsessions are ways we leave before we are left because we believe that the pain of staying would kill us.

But the person who would be killed, the "I" in the "pain is big and I am small" belief, is an idea, a memory, an image of yourself left over from childhood. You already felt destroyed. That was then. You will never be that small again. You are not dependent on someone else to hold you, to love you so that you can continue breathing.

Staying requires awareness of the desire to bolt. Of the stories you are telling yourself about the need to bolt. Staying means recognizing that when you want to bolt you are living in the past. You are taking yourself to be someone who no longer exists. Staying requires being curious about who you actually are when you don't take yourself to be a collection of memories. When you don't infer your existence from replaying what happened to you, when you don't take yourself to be the girl your mother/father/ brother/teacher/lover didn't see or adore. When you sense yourself directly, immediately, right now, without preconception, who are you?

When you stay, you question what you've never questioned: the you you take yourself to be. The you who is not your past, not your habits, not your compulsions. Anything becomes possible. Even living through extraordinary pain.

When I am afraid Matt will die when he walks out the door, I am afraid that I won't survive without him. When I want him to die to get it all over with, I want to stop the pain of anticipating the pain. As long as I believe that pain is bigger than me, as long as I define being open and vulnerable as being vulnerable to annihilation, I believe in an image of myself: that I am someone who can be annihilated. And when I believe this, I bolt from different situations by engaging in various mind-altering and body-numbing activities. I shut myself down or walk out the door when pain threatens to destroy me — which is in any situation that involves another human being or whose outcome I cannot control. I live an autistic existence.

But something else is happening as well: the refusal to accept — and therefore engage in — life as it is. In the way things are. People get old, get sick and die. Or they die suddenly. Or their deaths drag on forever. My friend Tory is dying a slow, excruciatingly painful death of bone cancer. Eight friends have died of breast cancer. Polar bears are dying. Honeybees are vanishing. The oceans are drying up. There is a part of me that wants my money back. That wants to say, "I didn't sign up for this. I don't like the way this whole thing is set up and I won't participate in it."

Stephen Levine, a Buddhist teacher, says that hell is wanting to be somewhere different from where you are. Being one place and wanting to be somewhere else. Being constantly agitated — another word for nonaccepting — about the inevitable. Being in a relationship with someone and refusing to surrender to the love because you don't want to give yourself to something you will eventually lose.

That's called living in hell: refusing to love because you want the endgame to be different than it is. Wanting life to be different from what it is.

That's also called leaving without leaving. Dying before you die. It's as if there is a part of you that so rails against being shattered by love that you shatter yourself first. Another name for this pattern? Obsession.

When one of the first things that happens at a retreat is that my students begin fighting with me, the setup of the retreat, the meeting times, I see this as the initial descent into (Stephen's definition of) hell: I'm here but I wish I wasn't. There must be an easier way. I want my money back. I don't like the rules of this game.

But the real "don't like" is: I don't like that I have this obsession with food and I don't want to do what I need to do to work with it. I thought I did but now that I'm here I've changed my mind. I'd rather go on another diet, I'd rather pretend that this is all about willpower and eating the right foods. I'd rather lose weight a thousand more times than truly see myself. Do the work of being aware of myself. Knowing myself. Discovering what I really believe about life, about love, about God.

The desire to leave the retreat is an expression of the desire to leave the obsession itself, to pretend that it's a minor problem that can be fixed in a few weeks with slight adjustments in exercise and portion control. It's a way of saying, "This is not my life, this is not my problem. There is no meaning for me here."

But as the days pass, the vortex of the retreat gets stronger, and something unexpected happens. My students give up the fight because they become aware of something they never thought existed: that which is beyond the pain. That which the pain passes through.

One student told me that she waited to come to a retreat for three years, until her kids were old enough for her to be away for five consecutive days. But when she finally arrived, she wanted to leave immediately. She dismissed what was happening, telling herself there was nothing new being taught. She called the airlines to check on a ticket home. She thought about taking a train.

About renting a car and driving cross-country.

She writes:

By the second day, I already felt jaded about what was happening here. I thought, "I know this already, this stuff is basic. I don't need to be here and I am not going to get anything out of it." I wanted to leave. But then I realized how my jadedness was actually resistance to staying with myself. Seeing this broke me open. I suddenly saw that that jaded attitude permeates my life. The dismissive attitude keeps me gravitating towards the spiritual pieces that are easy and accessible and feel-good. It keeps me protected from what I don't know. There is no mystery in the jadedness. No thrill of discovery. No real life.

The practice of bringing myself back to the present moment instead of careening around in my head is not one that comes easy to me. On the one hand I work myself so hard in my career that I feel justified in wanting an easy, relaxed, convenient spirituality. Spirituality that makes me feel better instantly. But I have had a shift here in seeing that real consistent practice of eating, breathing, showing up moment after moment — that is my true work. This is what a life can be. I see the commitment that staying will require, and I understand that it is not the same painful, shoulder-to-the-grindstone, vitality-squelching but approval-garnering work that I spend so much of my time doing. I see that doing this work requires humility and a willingness to return to myself, over and over and over. To be interested in what's actually here without the overlay of my past. But having now tasted what it's like to feel like my internal landscape is not strewn with land mines — that everything is truly workable and is in fact lovable and worthy of love — I don't want to go back to the way I lived before.

To stay, you have to believe there is something worth staying for — and then you have to bring yourself back, again and again. The initial glimpse of wonder, of love, of possibility, of expansion becomes a commitment to returning, to bringing yourself back each time you bolt.

I saw an interview recently with Stephen Levine (of the aforementioned hell definition) and his wife of thirty years, Ondrea. I met Stephen over dinner in Santa Cruz in 1978 when he was young and vital (and, um, so was I). He taught death-and-dying workshops, traveled everywhere, lectured to packed audiences of five hundred people or more. Now, he is so frail that he can't walk or make a fist with his hands. Ondrea has leukemia and is having seizures. Each of them said they weren't afraid of dying. Each of them said, "I'd like her/him to die first so that she doesn't have to suffer dying alone when I am gone."

Geez, I thought. This is a bit different from my crazy desire for Matt to die so that I can get the pain of anticipating his death over with. They want the other to die first; they are wishing for the pain of being left so that their partner will be spared that same pain. It's the opposite of bolting. It's walking straight into the pain with the understanding that there are worse things in life than a broken heart. That something exists beyond, something that completely saturates any pain. Something that holds the pain, is bigger than it is. And there is no fighting with either the pain or the thing that saturates it.

I realized then how much and with what I still fight: not just with death and loss. There is also the matter of my thighs that now look like yesterday's oatmeal or my neck that looks, as writer Anne Lamott says, like the

Utah desert is upholstered on it. I can't quite get over it. I'm in my fifties, and while I realize that's not old-old, I can't read labels in the grocery store without my glasses. The other day I bought a bar of chili chocolate instead of coffee chocolate. A grave offense. I realize that getting work done is always a possibility, but then I'd feel as if I was wearing a mask. Fighting the inevitable. Bolting from gravity. I say I believe in something deeper, something that doesn't die. And some of the time I call that something God. But every now and then I forget what I know and want to bolt all over again.

At some point, it's time to stop fighting with death, my thighs and the way things are. And to realize that emotional eating is nothing but bolting from multiple versions of the above: the obsession will stop when the bolting stops. And at that point, we might answer, as spiritual teacher Catherine Ingram did, when someone asked how she allowed herself to tolerate deep sorrow, "I live among the brokenhearted. They allow it."

# CHAPTER FOUR:
# IT'S NOT ABOUT THE
# WEIGHT BUT
# IT'S NOT NOT
# ABOUT THE WEIGHT

A few years ago, I received a letter from someone who'd included a Weight Watchers ribbon on which was embossed I LOST TEN POUNDS. Underneath the gold writing, the letter writer added, "And I Still Feel Like Crap."

We think we're miserable because of what we weigh. And to the extent that our joints hurt and our knees ache and we can't walk three blocks without losing our breath, we probably are physically miserable because of extra weight. But if we've spent the last five, twenty, fifty years obsessing about the same ten or twenty pounds, something else is going on. Something that has nothing to do with weight.

My friend Sally went to a wedding in Finland a few years ago and met a distant cousin of hers who was furious with me. The cousin said she'd read my books, followed my approach and gained a hundred pounds. She thought I was a charlatan, a fake, a louse. I didn't blame her. If I'd gained a hundred pounds while believing I was following an expert's advice, I'd be furious, too. A hundred pounds! My response to Sally's cousin was to say as kindly as I could — and with the safety of thousands of miles between us — that I realize she thought she was listening to me but I don't advocate eating compulsively. And gaining a hundred pounds is nothing but.

Most people are so glad to read about, hear about and then begin any approach that doesn't focus on weight loss as its main agenda that they take it to be license to eat without restraint. "Aha!" they say. "Someone finally understands that it's not about the weight." It's never been about the weight. It's not even about food. "Great," they say, "let's eat. A lot. Let's not stop."

And the truth is that it's not about the weight. It's never been about the weight. When a pill is discovered that allows people to eat whatever they want and not gain weight, the feelings and situations they turned to food to avoid will still be there, and they will find other more inventive ways to numb themselves. In *Groundhog Day,* when he realized he wasn't going to gain weight by eating a thousand cherry pies,

Bill Murray ate like there was no tomorrow (since, in the movie, there wasn't). But the charge dissipated as soon as he realized he could have as much food as he wanted without the usual consequences. When you take the charge away, all that's left is a no-big-deal piece of cherry pie. And when you finish the pie, the thing that had nothing to do with the pie — that drove you to it — is still there.

In the last year, I've gotten letters or worked with students who have

- mortgaged their houses to pay for a gastric bypass operation and then gained back the weight they lost.
- borrowed money — a lot of it — from a relative for liposuction and then discovered that they still hated their thighs.
- lost a hundred pounds and were so disappointed that it didn't fix what was broken that they gained back the weight.

Either you want to wake up or you want to go to sleep. You either want to live or you want to die.

It's not about the weight.

But it's also not *not* about the weight.

The reality of sheer poundage and its physical consequences cannot be denied. Some people at my retreats can't sit in a chair comfortably. They can't walk up a slight incline without feeling pain. Their doctors tell them their lives are in danger unless they lose weight. They need knee replacements, hip replacements, LAP-BAND surgeries. The pressure on their hearts, their kidneys, their joints is too much for their body to tolerate and still function well. So it *is* about the weight to the extent that weight gets in the way of basic function: of feeling, of doing, of moving, of being fully alive.

The in-your-face reality of the obesity epidemic — the fact that 75 percent of Americans are overweight — gets endless news coverage. Statistics about weight, the new drugs that are being discovered, the possibility of an obesity gene — all are discussed ad infinitum in the media. No one can argue that being a hundred pounds overweight is not physically challenging.

Yet.

The bottom line, whether you weigh 340 pounds or 150 pounds, is that when you eat when you are not hungry, you are using food as a drug, grappling with boredom or illness or loss or grief or emptiness or loneliness or rejection. Food is only the middle-man, the means to the end. Of altering your emotions. Of making yourself numb. Of creating a secondary problem when the original problem becomes too uncomfort-able. Of dying slowly rather than coming to terms with your messy, magnificent and very, very short — even at a hundred years old — life. The means to these ends hap-pens to be food, but it could be alcohol, it could be work, it could be sex, it could be cocaine. Surfing the Internet. Talking on the phone.

For a variety of reasons we don't fully understand (genetics, temperament, environment), those of us who are compul-sive eaters choose food. Not because of its taste. Not because of its texture or its color. We want quantity, volume, bulk. We need it — a lot of it — to go unconscious. To wipe out what's going on. The unconsciousness is what's important, not the food.

Sometimes people will say, "But I just like the taste of food. In fact, I love the taste! Why can't it be that simple? I overeat because I like food."

But.

When you like something, you pay atten-tion to it. When you like something — love something — you take time with it. You want to be present for every second of the rapture.

Overeating does not lead to rapture. It leads to burping and farting and being so sick that you can't think of anything but how full you are. That's not love; that's suffering.

Weight (too much or too little) is a by-product. Weight is what happens when you use food to flatten your life. Even with aching joints, it's not about food. Even with arthritis, diabetes, high blood pressure. It's about your desire to flatten your life. It's about the fact that you've given up without saying so. It's about your belief that it's not possible to live any other way — and you're using food to act that out without ever having to admit it.

This morning I received this letter:

Each time I start trying to follow what you say, I get afraid and then go running back to the security of the Weight Watchers point system. And every time I try points, I inevitably fail a week later and spiral into a new rash of binges and beating myself up.

My main concern is that I don't know how to face the actual deficiency in the rest of my life. I am a first-year associate at a large law firm in New York. By all accounts I am Going Places and will Be Something someday, but for now it's a lot of "skill-building" like managing nitty-gritty tasks and doing document review and never being able to sink my teeth into anything. I can manage my eating pretty well during the day, but at night I return home unsatisfied, and a binge results.

I can easily see the direct connection between this emptiness and my eating habits. Your books capture it perfectly. And I do just need to stare my frustration with my job and my career in the face instead of distracting myself from it with food. I just don't know how to deal with this when I have to be in this job, at a minimum, another eight months (to get my bonus) and likely another twelve months, until my boyfriend completes his stint and we can think about moving somewhere else. Intellectually, I can reconcile being in this job with an overall career arc, but on a day-to-day basis, it's just aggravating.

I guess I'm writing this more so I can disabuse these binges of their power, but even with this clarity I am not sure I can really make paying attention to hunger a sustainable pattern if this job continues to sap me of my energy.

So what's a girl to do when she is destined to be Someone but in the meantime feels as if she is No One Special? How does she face what she doesn't want to face without eating? That's really the dilemma. "I don't want to be where I am and so I am eating to wipe out the 'aggravation.' How can I feel the aggravation without eating to make myself feel better?"

Let's suppose that she keeps eating. Every night she comes home and binges. Soon she gains weight, then more weight. Perhaps she gains so much weight that her joints ache, her back hurts, the pressure on her knees becomes painful and then excruciating. Instead of worrying about being No One, she is now worried about getting her knees replaced. She has joined the ranks of the obese, and it looks to her and all the world that the problem is her weight. That if she could only lose weight, her body would function well (this is probably true) and she would be happy (this is not true). But her problem is not about the food she consumes. Her problem, though it eventually would become excess weight, is not weight. It's that she doesn't know — no one ever taught her — how to "face" (as she calls it) her "deficiency." The emptiness. The dissatisfaction.

I see four choices. The first is to keep doing what she is doing. That's the choice that most of us make most of the time. Caught in a conundrum, in a paradox — "I need to stay here but I don't want to. Staying here makes me unhappy. Being unhappy makes me eat" — we usually make a hoopla out of compulsive eating and call that The Problem. Our lack of willpower, our nightly binges, our expanding body sizes. And while, with enough weight gain, it really does become a problem that needs to be addressed, it's a problem we've manufactured so we don't have to deal with the unknown.

Her second choice is to leave her job and find something she wants to do now. A more difficult choice, especially if being an attorney is her passion, which, at the beginning, requires working at tasks that don't thrill her.

And her third choice — the one with which she is grappling — is to untangle the knot she is calling "deficiency." To demystify the emptiness she runs away from night after night. If the nighttime feelings were no longer frightening, there'd be no need to turn to a drug to numb them.

Deficiency. Emptiness. They're just words, names that evoke scary thoughts, which

75

then evoke scary feelings. And both the thoughts and the feelings are based on her idea of what is supposed to be happening that isn't: "I'm supposed to be Someone Special and here I am doing grunt work and reviewing other people's documents. This isn't what I dreamed about. I'm never going to amount to anything. My life is a waste. What if it's always like this? What if my dreams are just pipe dreams? I should have known this was going to happen. I should have listened to my eighth-grade teacher, Mrs. Simpkinson, when she told me I'd never amount to anything. Oh, I feel so empty. I feel deficient, flawed, like I am and never will be enough. I need to eat."

Deficiency sounds awful, but is it? What does it actually feel like? Is it a big hole in her stomach? Her chest? Does it feel like everything has dropped away and she's holding on to the edge of a huge abyss, about to fall in? If she stops trying to hold on and lets herself fall, what would happen? (Remember that all of these are images in her mind. She's not really holding on to the edge of an abyss, she's probably sitting in a chair. She wouldn't actually fall anywhere if, in her mind, she let herself "fall.") Is emptiness the experience of space or is it something else? If it's space and she feels it directly — in her body where it resides — she might notice if there is anything that is actually scary about it or if it's just a story she is telling herself.

There is a whole universe to discover between "I'm feeling empty" and turning to food to make it go away. The problem of weight is predictable. We know what to do when we have that problem. Beat ourselves up. Make ourselves wrong. Eat fewer donuts. But staying with the emptiness — entering it, welcoming it, using it to get to know ourselves better, being able to distinguish the stories we tell ourselves about it from the actual feeling itself — that's radical.

Imagine not being frightened by any feeling. Imagine knowing that nothing will destroy you. That you are beyond any feeling, any state. Bigger than. Vaster than. That there is no reason to use drugs because anything a drug could do would pale in comparison to knowing who you are. To what you can understand, live, be, just by being with what presents itself to you in the form of the feelings you have when you get home from work at night.

Her fourth choice: accepting the situation. Dropping the resistance to doing grunt work. Understanding that this is the way things are for now and being vigilant about bringing her attention to the present moment again and again.

Acceptance represents the basic challenge of compulsive eating. The reason why it's not about the weight. Why people Lose Ten Pounds and Still Feel Like Crap.

The lack of acceptance and the lawyer's unhappiness are synonymous. She is assuming — absolutely counting on the fact — that when she gets to be Someone Special, she will no longer feel deficient and no longer be haunted by emptiness. I've thought that, too. About a hundred million times. It's called the "When I Get Thin (Change Jobs, Move, Find a Relationship, Leave This Relationship, Have Money) Blues." It's called the "If Only" refrain. It's called postponing your life and your ability to be happy to a future date when then, oh then, you will finally get what you want and life will be good. In my books *Feeding the Hungry Heart* and *When Food Is Love,* I've written about the stories of people who lost weight and were still miserable. Who got what they thought they wanted most and found that joy still eluded them. Because — and yes, I know this is a cliché but it's a cliché because it's actually true — miserable and happy are not functions of what you

78

have, what you look like or what you achieve. I'm not exactly proud to say that I have been miserable anywhere, with anything, with anyone. I've been miserable standing in a field of a thousand sunflowers in southern France in mid-June. I've been miserable weighing eighty pounds and wearing a size 0. And I've been happy wearing a size 18. Happy sitting with my dying father. Happy being a switchboard operator.

It's not about the weight. It's not about the goal. It's not about Being Thin or Being Someone Special or Getting There. Those are fantasies in your mind — and they are all in the future, a future that never comes. Because when your goals are reached, they will be reached in the "right now." And in the "right now," you will still be you, doing the same things you do now. You will still stand up. Walk around. Get root canals. Open the refrigerator door. Sleep. Feel happy. Feel devastated. Feel lonely. Feel loved. Get old. Die.

But it's not *not* about the weight because if you keep using food as a drug, if you keep distracting yourself by creating a weight problem, then you need to attend to your weight in order to stand up, walk around, open doors, sleep, feel happy, feel devastated, feel loved, get old, die — with any degree of attention, wholeheartedness, presence. If you keep slapping another problem on top of the freshness of life itself, all you see is what you've slapped on to it. You cannot ignore a problem just because it's one you've manufactured.

At some point, it becomes about the weight. When you can't live the rest of your life with ease, the weight itself needs to be addressed. Not so that you can become super-model thin. Not so that you can look like an image in your mind that has nothing to do with your body, your age, your life. You need to address the weight because without addressing it, you don't actually live. You schlep yourself from place to place, out of breath. Sitting is painful. Flying is torturous. Going to the movies is challenging. You become so burdened with the problem you've created that your life becomes small and your focus becomes narrow. Life becomes about your limitations. What you can and cannot do. How much you can hide. How ashamed you are of yourself. You close down your senses, you leave the world of sounds, of color, of laughter in favor of a reality you've created yourself. If you keep using food as a drug, if your life becomes about your weight, you miss everything that is not related to your weight problem. You die without ever having lived.

Here is the letter I wrote to No One in Particular who is hoping to be Someone Special and creating a weight problem in the meantime.

It seems as if you chose this career and therefore this career arc. Can you accept that? Not as resignation, which is how people define acceptance. Not as a sense of victimhood: "Poor me, I can't do anything but accept the situation." But as the willingness to stop defining your tasks as a means to an end and instead inhabit what you yourself have chosen. What if this is exactly what you are supposed to be doing because it is what you are doing? What if each nitty-gritty task is perfection itself and you keep missing it because you're looking for something else?

It's like washing the dishes. If you focus on getting the dishes done so that your kitchen will be clean, you miss everything that happens between dirty and clean. The warmth of the water, the pop of the bubbles, the movements of your hand. You miss the life that happens in the middle zone — between now and what you think your life should be like. And when you miss those moments because you'd rather be doing something else, you are missing your own life. Those moments are gone. You will never get them back.

Even when you become Something because they were right, you really were Going Places — even when you arrive at being Someone because you are where you were going — your life may not be any better if you haven't learned to be awake, alive, now. To take this moment for what it is. It's just as easy to be miserable when you are Someone Special as when you are No One in Particular. Because even Someone Special still has to live in her own skin and deal with boredom, rejection, loneliness, disappointment. Even Someone Special comes home at night and does what the Nobodies do: falls asleep alone. You might as well learn how to pay attention now. How to inhabit the life you've chosen. How to take up every inch of your skin. Occupy the space in this body you were given. It's your place. Only yours.

The writer Annie Dillard says, "How you spend your days is how you spend your life." Be unwaveringly honest. Ask yourself how you want to spend your days. Since you're going to be reviewing documents anyway, why not be aware of your breath and the ticking clock while you are doing it?

Whatever it offers, the reality of your day-to-day life has to be better than the self-inflicted misery you are creating through the stories you are telling yourself. It has to be better than the nightly binges and throwing yourself into the cycle of self-loathing and promises to stop eating so much.

Come back. Break the trance. Pay attention to your breath. Your arms. Your legs. Listen to sounds. The scrape of a chair. The whirr of the copy machine. Notice colors. The royal blue of a coworker's dress. The coffee stain on your boss's tie. Wake up to the riot of life around you every second. The singer Pearl Bailey said, "People see God every day; they just don't recognize Him." What if every day was a chance to see a new version of God? What if what you needed was right in front of you and you were not recognizing it?

You already have everything you need to be content. Your real work, despite the corporate ladder you are climbing, is to do whatever it takes to realize that. And then it won't matter if you're Someone Special or No One in Particular because you'll be fully alive in every moment — which is, I imagine, all you ever wanted from Going Places to be Someone.

Or from being thin.

# Chapter Five:
## Beyond What's
### Broken

Somewhere along the line I started believing that the purpose of living was to pass the test I'd be given when I died. At the moment of my last breath, there would be a judgment hearing at which I'd be forced to review my life. Given my propensities toward taking the biggest piece of anything and amassing large quantities of earrings when so much of the world lived on less than a dollar a day, there would be no doubt about the verdict: I was going to hell. Unless, of course, I spent the remaining days of my life trying to be selfless like Mother Teresa and go without lip gloss. Or, at the very least, gave away all my material possessions and lived in a house made of grass, sleeping on a mattress made of hemp, wearing clothes made of recycled bottles and eating a diet of beneficial microorganisms found in dirt.

When I first meet people who come to my

retreat, I see those same beliefs funneled through the relationship with food. As if punishing themselves with dietary rigors will make up for something inherently damaged, fundamentally wrong with their very existence. Being thin becomes The Test. Losing weight becomes their religion. They must suffer humiliation and torment, they must enroll in an endless succession of dietary privations, and then and only then will they be pure, be holy, be saved.

When I was on Weight Watchers in the early seventies, I was staying at a friend's house for a week. They would sit down to their meals of meat loaf and mashed potatoes and I would sit down to whatever was on my diet. One evening, I made dinner out of the remaining allowable foods for the day: two servings of cold tomato sauce — using the stove was not one of my specialties — and a serving of ricotta cheese. I was scooping my dinner into a bowl when my friend Alan said to me, "Is that really what you want to eat? Cold tomato sauce with a lump of cold cheese?" "Yes," I said, "of course." But the truth was that "No" was not an option. Eating what I wanted was not allowed. Wanting what I wanted was not allowed. I needed to sacrifice, atone, make up for being myself.

For being fat.

The most difficult part of teaching people to respect and listen to their bodies is overcoming their conviction that there is nothing to respect. They can't find any place in them that is whole or intact. And so when they hear me say, "Relax," when they hear me say, "Trust yourself," they feel as if I am asking them to throw themselves to the wolves. Banishing them to wild and ferocious brokenness. The possibility that there is a place in them, in everyone, that is unbroken, that has never gained a pound, never been hungry, never been wounded, seems like a myth as far-fetched as the Sumerian goddess Inanna ascending to earth after hanging on a meat hook in hell. But then I ask them about babies. I ask them to remember their own children and how they come into the world already gorgeous and utterly deserving of love. They nod their heads. They realize that brokenness is learned, not innate, and that their work is to find their way back to what is already whole.

A few months ago I lost my face. It wasn't the "Honey, I lost my car keys" kind of losing; I woke up one morning to find that my face had been replaced by a beach ball–sized orb, a wavy hole beneath my nose formerly known as my mouth, and two swollen protrusions below my forehead out of which the slits of my erstwhile crescent-shaped eyes could see. Red oozy bumps — the result of an allergic reaction earlier in the week — occupied the area where my skin had recently lived.

And since our biannual retreat was in its second of six days, and since its remote location made it impossible to leave and return for medical attention in time for the next session, there was nothing to do but spend the week facing a hundred people without my face.

On the third day, my face was twice the size as the day before and the bumps now felt like a thousand stinging bees. On the fourth day, I could only open one eye. "Is it hard to look at me?" I asked one of my co-teachers. "Yes," he said. "Do I look deformed?" "Uh-huh," he said. "Like Elephant Man. But only when I first see you. Then I get used to it."

I wish I could say that I accepted my new look with unclouded equanimity and Buddha-like serenity. But my constitutional predilections toward drama and hysteria propelled me in their well-trodden grooves.

I touched my face at thirty-second intervals to see if it had gotten better; I caused myself immense suffering by refusing to believe this was happening. I wanted my face back. *Now.* It wasn't fair. It wasn't that I disagreed with the idea of loss. Or that certain losses — death, for example — were part of life. But losing my face? That was going too far.

When I saw anything that breathed — a person, a dog, a lizard — I thought, *You still have your face, what could you have to complain about?* I thought about all the people with facial deformities. About the real Elephant Man. I thought, *If I ever get my face back, I will never take my cheeks for granted. I will never complain about the crow's-feet, never have one more speck of disregard about the sun spots, the wrinkles and their offspring.* I will wake up every morning and greet my countenance with enthusiasm and gratitude, as if it was as miraculous as the virgin birth.

And then slowly, because I was teaching a retreat on looking below the surface of things, I began to notice that nothing was actually wrong. The noticing was grudging at first, as if I was a three-year-old throwing a tantrum about losing her favorite doll and had become quite fond of making a ruckus despite having found the doll. I inhabited my misery as if it was a well-worn coat. Because I could. Because I knew how. Because it had kept me company during the early years. But the more I noticed that I could no longer use my face as my logo — the locus of whatever made me me — the freer I felt. Without my face, my identity became undone. When I couldn't pretend to be someone special, when I could no longer coagulate the different parts of myself into a mask that looked cohesive and in control, an unexpected freshness whooshed through the door.

It was like those times when I can't sleep and I am thrashing in bed, hot and sweaty and wound in a knot of feverish mental activity. A thought enters like a prayer: *Go outside. Walk out the front door and look at the sky. Just for a minute. Listen to the night.* If I can rouse myself from the hypnotic trance of what's wrong, I throw a sweater on, pad to the door, and step into the vault of night. Coolness. Silence. A million points of glitter. Heart beats once, twice, three times. The mind sloughs its frenzy, merges with the expanse. Dazzled by a world that bears no resemblance to the one of ten minutes ago, the one I perpetually construct in my head, I slip back into the house as if I, too, am a pinpoint of luster from the

90

boundless dimension, padding along some strange hallway, disappearing with each step until I fall back asleep.

While I was without my face, when compassion was needed, it arose. When it was time for me to give a talk, talking happened. Everything that needed to happen — feeling, laughing, crying, thinking, sleeping, sitting, walking, eating, tasting, swallowing — happened without my face. Something I didn't normally call me was still there, although the physical apparatus I had most associated with being me was gone. This is what all the spiritual hoo-ha is about, I thought. This unbreakable presence, this loss-proof wholeness. This is what must be left after everything that can die is dead and everything that can be lost is gone.

Since I was already at the retreat, I decided to use my face as part of the teaching. I asked my students what they saw when they looked at me. Did they believe that I was still me without my face? Mostly I wanted them to use their reactions to my face as a way to explore what they believed about their bodies. If they gained ten pounds, if their arms didn't look the way they wanted them to look, were they still themselves? Besides the ongoing story in their minds about the way it should be, the way they wanted it to be, the way it needed to be for them to be happy, was anything actually wrong? What remained when they lost their ideas of what they believed they couldn't live without?

Months before, we'd done a mirror exercise together. I'd asked each of them to walk up to the full-length mirror and tell me what they saw. The litanies of judgments were all very similar. "I see humongous thighs." "I see flat stringy hair." "I see a horrible double chin." "I see arms that hang down to Montana." "I see cellulite — it's disgusting — poking through my pants." "I can't stand what I see. I can't stand looking at myself." *My body and I are one. There is nothing good about my body and therefore there is nothing good about me.*

Then I asked them to look again at their bodies, beginning with their eyes. I asked them to look beyond the color and shape of their eyes and to see what was seeing. For people who didn't quite understand the seeing-what-was-seeing part, I asked them to remember, if only for a moment, what it was like to be a child before they began to label and name the objects in their world. What it was like to see an extravaganza of form and color before they knew it was a rose and could compare it to other roses. What it was like to come upon a treasure, any treasure — a rock, the ocean, their mother's hand — before they learned to label and dismiss it as something they already knew.

Everyone immediately understood what I was saying, as if I was speaking a secret language they'd been waiting to speak without realizing they'd been waiting. When they walked up to the mirror, they used words like *brilliance*, like *precious*, like *completely open*. "I see wonder," one person said. "I see innocence." People saw beauty and loveliness and a feast of color and shape when they looked at their faces, the legs that carried them, the arms that held their children. One woman, after a profusion of near ecstatic adjectives about her body (and what was seeing her body), said to me, "Geneen! Are you hypnotizing me?" She didn't remember, in all her adult life, looking at herself with anything but disdain. I told her that I believed she'd already been hypnotized — and that hating herself was the result.

At our About Face retreat, most everyone said they didn't actually notice my face for more than a passing moment. A face, it seems, is only the entry point to what is beyond it. To what one student called "the essence of the essence." (Not everyone was so lofty. One person said, "Oh, an allergic reaction! I was wondering why you looked so haggard and old.")

"And is that how you feel about your bodies? That it's the entry point to what's beyond it? To some sort of essence?" I asked.

*Not so much. Not really. No way. Are you joking?*

Someone said, "What if I'm missing the essential part? What if I really am broken through and through?"

"It's not possible," I told her. "Look again." Then I told her the story of the Sufi dervish called Mullah Nasrudin, who was smuggling treasure across the border and masterfully eluding the guards. Every day for four years he would parade back and forth, and with every crossing the guards knew he was hiding expensive goods that he would sell for outrageous amounts of money on the other side. But despite their thorough searches, and despite the fact that they could see that he was prospering, they could find nothing in the saddle of the donkey he rode. Finally, years later, after Nasrudin had moved to another county, the frontier guard said, "Okay, you can tell me now. What were you smuggling?" Nasrudin smiled broadly.

94

"My dear friend," he said, "I was smuggling donkeys."

It's hidden in plain sight. The open secret. Every day we are in touch with that which is not broken. But we are so busy paying attention to the million details of day-to-day life that we miss it. Whether we name it or not, it is still there. Whether we pay attention to it or not, it doesn't go away.

Think about a time when you were transported beyond what you normally define as yourself. When time stopped. When you felt the edges of ordinary life dissolve and a door open to another dimension. Maybe it happened only once, when you were in the middle of a rain forest or gave birth to your child. Maybe it happened when you were twenty and on drugs. Maybe it happens whenever you are in nature or when, for no reason, you are suddenly happy. Five minutes ago you were dragging your feet. The sun was too hot. Your kids were screeching or your boss was yelling and you hated your life. And suddenly you caught a glimpse of beauty and it's as if someone opened the cage door and let you out of the iron vise of your mind. And not one thing has changed from the moment before but everything looks and feels and is completely different.

Among its many other motivations, compulsive eating is a reaching for, a yearning for, an attempt to contact the place that is already whole. When you ask people who are yoked to disordered eating about their motivations for turning to food, they say things like "I want peace. Quiet. To forget about myself for a while. To go into another zone." It's as if the knowledge of the expanse beyond the concerns of the personal is already there and they are using food to access it. Which — no surprise — leads to more pain. Because although the attempt may be honorable, the means to reach it causes alienation, isolation, suffering.

Eventually, we get so tired of trying to fix ourselves that we stop. We see that we've never been able to make ourselves good. Never been able to accomplish ourselves into being someone else. And so we stop trying. We see there is no goal, no end place, no test to take. No one is keeping score. No one is watching us and deciding whether we are worthy enough to ascend. As one of my teachers once said, "You can't be stuck if you're not trying to get anywhere." Eventually we see that it was the investment in the brokenness, the constant effort to fix ourselves, that was the very thing that kept the wholeness at bay. If you think that your job is to fix what is broken, you keep finding more broken places to mend. It's better than being out of a job. Especially in this economy.

From one of my students:

During the retreat, I realized how much I have done to make up for being myself. How much I have strived and efforted to counter what I believe is wrong. I realize that no one is fundamentally damaged — that every baby is born with an intact sense of being themselves — but the architecture of my nervous system seems to be skewed in a particular direction: I have to make up for being myself. I can't listen to impulses because if I (the damaged one) am having them, they must be damaged. And therefore, I have to do exactly what I don't want to do because if it's hard, if I suffer, it must be the right thing. The hardness, the suffering will somehow clean the slate, cleanse the damage.

So much of my longing to "awaken" has come from a desire to be good. Like there's a big mother in the sky who is watching what I do and giving me gold stars for getting up every day and meditating. For working on myself so much, so hard, and for so many years. I feel as if I need to find out what I am doing for self-expression, and what I am doing for self-improvement. What I am doing because it's an effulgence and what I am doing to get something that I don't believe I have, to be someone I don't believe I am. I tired enough of the search — and not finding anything — that I am giving it up. It's scary to say that. It's kind of like the moment I gave up dieting. I felt as if I was committing a sin by announcing to the world/ myself that I could trust myself. Now it's a different kind of giving up: the attempt to atone for being born as me. But I am ready. I can feel it in my bones. I no longer believe that I am broken. Or that if I am, there is any way of fixing it.

Of this I am certain: something happens every time I stop fighting with the way things are. Something happens to every one of my students when they stop running their familiar programs about fear and deficiency and emptiness. I don't know what to call this turn of events or the freshness that follows it, but I know what it feels like: it feels like relief. It feels like infinite goodness. Like a distillation of every sweet fragrance, every heartstopping beauty, every haunting melody you've ever heard. It feels like the essence of tenderness, compassion, joy, peace. Like love itself. And in the moment you feel it you recognize that you *are* it and that you've been here all along, waiting for your return.

When you forget, which you always do, you suddenly understand that kindness to anyone — a plant, an animal, a stranger, a partner — brings you closer to this. That taking care of your body is taking care of this. That taking care of the earth is taking care of this. And that you'd turn away from anything or anyone that asked you to leave this because this is what you've wanted, this is what you've longed for, this is what you've loved for eons. You know without knowing how you know that every step you've ever taken, every person you've ever loved, every task you've ever accomplished has been This meeting This. You returning to yourself. And that hell is nothing more than leaving this. Heaven is already here on earth.

# CHAPTER SIX:
# RETEACHING
# LOVELINESS

When I was in high school, I used to dream about having Melissa Morris's legs, Toni Oliver's eyes and Amy Breyer's hair. I liked my skin, my breasts and my lips but everything else had to go. Then, in my twenties, I dreamed about slicing off pieces of my thighs and arms the way you carve a turkey, certain that if I could cut away what was wrong, only the good parts — the pretty parts, the thin parts — would be left.

I believed there was an end goal, a place at which I would arrive and forevermore be at peace. And since I also believed that the way to get there was by judging and shaming and hating myself, I also believed in diets.

Diets are based on the unspoken fear that you are a madwoman, a food terrorist, a lunatic. Eventually you will destroy all that you love and so you need to be stopped. The promise of a diet is not only that you will have a different body; it is that in having a different body, you will have a different life. If you hate yourself enough, you will love yourself. If you torture yourself enough, you will become a peaceful, relaxed human being.

Although the very notion that hatred leads to love and that torture leads to relaxation is absolutely insane, we hypnotize ourselves into believing that the end justifies the means. We treat ourselves and the rest of the world as if deprivation, punishment and shame lead to change. We treat our bodies as if they are the enemy and the only acceptable outcome is annihilation. Our deeply ingrained belief is that hatred and torture work. And although I've never met anyone — not one person — for whom warring with their bodies led to long-lasting change, we continue to believe that with a little more self-disgust, we'll prevail.

A talk show host once asked me how people could change their relationships with food. When I answered that understanding was the first step, he said, "That's it? That's all? We're supposed to believe that change happens by going around *understanding* ourselves?"

Yes, as the first step. Because until you

101

understand who you take yourself to be, true change is not possible. Even if you are lucky enough to get every single thing you think you want, the person who gets those things — your sense of yourself — will still be poverty-stricken and miserable and fat.

You can be showered with money or love or thin thighs and still feel as if you are separate from all that is good about being alive. Despite present-day circumstances, your deepest beliefs will always — 100 percent of the time — reconfigure you into the familiar patterns you associate with being yourself. Being at your natural weight will be impossible to maintain. Having what you want will not seem real. When someone truly loves you, you will dismiss her or him as unattractive or shallow or dumb. You will feel like an imposter living someone else's life. And you will once again inhabit the skin and the life of unlove in whatever forms you find most familiar.

Until you understand that you are oriented toward damage and doom, toward being wedded to compulsive eating and all its problems, until you realize that you insist upon it, albeit unconsciously, no change will last because you will be working against your natural tendencies. You will be overriding your deepest convictions about being alive.

The shape of your body obeys the shape of your beliefs about love, value and possibility. To change your body, you must first understand that which is shaping it. Not fight it. Not force it. Not deprive it. Not shame it. Not do anything but accept — and, yes, Virginia — understand it. Because if you force and deprive and shame yourself into being thin, you end up a deprived, shamed, fearful person who will also be thin for ten minutes. When you abuse yourself (by taunting or threatening yourself) you become a bruised human being no matter how much you weigh. When you demonize yourself, when you pit one part of you against another — your ironclad will against your bottomless hunger — you end up feeling split and crazed and afraid that the part you locked away will, when you are least prepared, take over and ruin your life. Losing weight on any program in which you tell yourself that left to your real impulses you would devour the universe is like building a skyscraper on sand: without a foundation, the new structure collapses.

Change, if it is to be long lasting, must occur on the unseen levels first. With understanding, inquiry, openness. With the realization that you eat the way you do for lifesaving reasons.

I tell my retreat students that there are *always* exquisitely good reasons why they turn to food. Unless they assume that they are fundamentally sane and that what they are doing makes perfect sense — and that their job is to discover the unspoken, the unseen, the unknown patterns to which they conform and not push themselves in a direction their minds have decided they must pursue — they will be at war with themselves no matter what they weigh. It's the belief in war we focus on, not the weight, because once the belief is gone, the weight will follow.

Our work is not to change what you do, but to witness what you do with enough awareness, enough curiosity, enough tenderness that the lies and old decisions upon which the compulsion is based become apparent and fall away. When you no longer believe that eating will save your life when you feel exhausted or overwhelmed or lonely, you will stop. When you believe in yourself more than you believe in food, you will stop using food as if it were your only chance at not falling apart. When the shape of your body no longer matches the shape of your beliefs, the weight disappears. And yes, it really is that simple.

You will stop turning to food when you start understanding in your body, not just your mind, that there is something better than turning to food. And this time, when you lose weight, you will keep it off.

Truth, not force, does the work of ending compulsive eating.

Awareness, not deprivation, informs what you eat.

Presence, not shame, changes how you see yourself and what you rely on.

When you stop struggling, stop suffering, stop pushing and pulling yourself around food and your body, when you stop manipulating and controlling, when you actually relax and listen to the truth of what is there, something bigger than your fear will catch you. With repeated experiences of opening and ease, you learn to trust something infinitely more powerful than a set of rules that someone else made up: your own being.

The poet Galway Kinnell wrote that "sometimes it is necessary to reteach a thing its loveliness."

Everything we do, I tell my students, is to reteach ourselves our loveliness.

■ ■ ■ ■

After I stopped dieting and my weight normalized, some of the beliefs that fueled my relationship with food resurfaced in the relentless drive to succeed and the inability to rest or to take satisfaction in what I did or had or loved.

No matter what I thought or did or wrote, they were the wrong thoughts, the wrong books. If I was unhappy, if I was longing for something I didn't have, if someone else had it (whatever *it* was) and I didn't, I knew who I was.

Where others saw dawn, I saw doom. Where they saw love, I saw boredom. Where they saw peace, I saw suffocation. Contentment made me nervous. Happiness made me anxious on a level I couldn't explain. But letting go of the misery felt as if I was letting go of the world as I knew it. It felt as if I was betraying the child who'd grown up desperate and fat and lonely.

When my unspoken marriage to unhappiness began to surface through the practices I describe in the book, I was already married to Matt and had more financial and worldly success than 95 percent of the world. You would never have known by looking at me what was below the surface. But I'd find myself staring at my husband and thinking, Who are you? I hate those pants, the way you chew cereal. And why exactly did I marry you? Then I'd look around at my friends, my community, my life and feel that I didn't belong in my own skin.

When you believe without knowing you believe that you are damaged at your core, you also believe that you need to hide that damage for anyone to love you. You walk around ashamed of being yourself. You try hard to make up for the way you look, walk, feel. Decisions are agonizing because if you, the person who makes the decision, is damaged, then how can you trust what you decide? You doubt your own impulses so you become masterful at looking outside yourself for comfort. You become an expert at finding experts and programs, at striving and trying hard and then harder to change yourself, but this process only reaffirms what you already believe about yourself — that your needs and choices cannot be trusted, and left to your own devices you are out of control.

Diets are the outpicturing of your belief that you have to atone for being yourself to be worthy of existing. They are not the source of this belief, they are only one expression of it. Until the belief is understood and questioned, no amount of weight loss will touch the part of you that is convinced it is damaged. A lifetime of suffering with food will fit right in with the definition you've formed about being alive. It will make sense to you that hatred leads to love and that torture leads to peace because you will be operating on the conviction that you must starve or deprive or punish the badness out of you. You won't keep extra weight off because being at your natural weight does not match your convictions about the way life unfolds. But once the belief and the subsequent decisions are questioned, diets and being uncomfortable in your body lose their seductive allure. Only kindness makes sense. Anything else is excruciating.

You are not a mistake. You are not a problem to be solved. But you won't discover this until you are willing to stop banging your head against the wall of shaming and caging and fearing yourself. The Sufi poet Rumi, writing about birds learning to fly, wrote: "How do they learn it? They fall, and falling, they're given wings."

If you wait until you have Toni Oliver's

eyes and Amy Breyer's hair, if you wait to respect yourself until you are at the weight you imagine you need to be to respect yourself, you will never respect yourself, because the message you will be giving yourself as you reach your goal is that you are damaged and cannot trust your impulses, your longings, your dreams, your essence at any weight.

A retreat student recently wrote:

The changes in my body (I've lost twenty-five pounds and that is the least of it) do not begin to express the changes in my life. It is a steady journey of remembering . . . of feeling alive instead of more like the walking dead . . . of actually experiencing moments, wonderful, glorious moments of true joy (and I don't use that word easily or often), . . . of feeling the surge of pride, strength and hope that come when I am often able to stay with my feelings instead of going into automatic pilot and plunging into food . . . of being able to treat myself with gentleness, kindness and compassion instead of feeling like a whipping post . . . and the ultimate treasure for me . . . of being able to feel love for myself — and from that love, for my children, my partner, people on the streets. For so many years, I knew how important loving myself was, yet could only access the idea through my intellect, never my heart.

Either you are willing to believe in kindness or you aren't. Either you are willing to believe in the basic sanity of your being or you aren't. To be given wings, you've got to be willing to believe that you were put on this earth for more than your endless attempts to lose the same thirty pounds three hundred times for eighty years. And that goodness and loveliness are possible, even in something as mundane as what you put in your mouth for breakfast. Beginning now.

Once you take the first few steps, once you begin treating yourself with the kindness that you believe only thin or perfect people deserve, you can't help but discover that love didn't abandon you after all.

■ ■ ■ ■

# Part Two:
# Practices

■ ■ ■ ■

# Chapter Seven:
# Tigers in the Mind

No matter how developed you are in any other area of your life, no matter what you say you believe, no matter how sophisticated or enlightened you think you are, how you eat tells all.

Bummer.

But think of it this way: the desire to eat when you are not hungry reveals what you truly believe about life here on earth — your panoply of beliefs about feeling, suffering, receiving, nourishing, abundance, resting, having enough. And once you know what you believe, you can begin to question if it is true.

In the moment that you reach for potato chips to avoid what you feel, you are effectively saying, "I have no choice but to numb myself. Some things can't be felt, understood or worked through." You are saying, "There is no possibility of change so I might as well eat." You are saying, "Goodness exists for everyone but me so I might as well eat." You are saying, "I am fundamentally flawed so I might as well eat." Or, "Food is the only true pleasure in life so I might as well eat."

When you first begin questioning your core beliefs, you don't try to fix or change or improve them. You take a breath, then you take another. You notice sensations in your body, if there is tingling or pulsing or warmth or coolness. You notice what you feel, and even if you have always called this feeling "sadness," you are curious about it as if there is no word associated with it, no label describing it, as if it is the first time you have ever encountered it. Is it a lump of blue burned ashes in your chest? Does it feel like a hole in your heart? When you notice it, does it open or change?

This kind of questioning provides a bridge between who you take yourself to be and who you actually are. Between what you tell yourself based on stories from your past and what you sense based on your direct experience now. It allows you to distinguish between outdated familiar patterns and the current, living truth.

I spent years in therapy, years in various kinds of meditation practice. I knew how to

muck around in the wounds of my childhood and I knew how to transcend them,
how to heal the pain of being abused and
how to contact the part of me that was
never abused. But when I got done meditating and soaring around in resplendence, I'd
clunk back into the day-to-day world of my
personality as if the two were not connected. Although carryover was one of the
promised benefits of meditation, I was failing miserably. Put me in the middle of an
argument and my thirty-minutes-a-day
serenity was instantly replaced by my default, well-grooved beliefs: trust no one; love
hurts; if I don't grab it all now, there won't
be anything left for me.

Meditating was teaching me how to transcend my life, but I wanted to learn how to
live in it. And I wanted, as William James
said, to do it flamboyantly and starting now.
"No exceptions."

Then, as a student of the Diamond Approach, I learned a version of inquiry — a
philosophical/scientific/psychological/
spiritual process that has been around in
various forms for thousands of years. The
version I learned was body-based and
always began in the present moment, with
my direct experience. My teacher, Jeanne
Hay, said, "You're trying too hard, you're

working too much, you've been in therapy too long." She said, "Instead of trying to change it all, start noticing what's already here. Pay attention to what you already feel. Sad. Bored. Happy. Hungry. Miserable. Ecstatic." She said that if I was curious about the big chunks of flying objects (my old beliefs) that were taking up my attention, they would change, open, dissolve.

I didn't believe her at first. This kind of inquiry requires inhabiting a feeling completely, and I thought, as my students now do, that I would drown in sadness, be consumed with anger. I thought that keeping the feelings away was what was allowing me to function and that in practicing inquiry I'd be unable to cope.

But it turns out that being with feelings is not the same as drowning in them. With awareness (the ability to know what you are feeling) and presence (the ability to inhabit a feeling while sensing that which is bigger than the feeling), it is possible to be with what you believe will destroy you without being destroyed. It is possible to be with big heaves of feelings like grief or terror. Little waves of feelings like crankiness or sadness.

The path from obsession to feelings to presence is not about healing our "wounded children" or feeling every bit of rage or grief we never felt so that we can be successful, thin, and happy. We are not trying to put ourselves together. We are taking who we think we are apart. We feel the feelings not so that we can blame our parents for not saying, "Oh darling," not so that we can hit pillows and express our anger to everyone we've never confronted, but because unmet feelings obscure our ability to know ourselves. As long as we take ourselves to be the child who was hurt by an unconscious parent, we will never grow up. We will never know who we actually are. We will keep looking for the parent who never showed up and forget to see that the one who is looking is no longer a child.

Catherine Ingram tells a story in her book *Passionate Presence* about a young friend of hers who said, "Pretend you are surrounded by a thousand hungry tigers. What would you do?" Catherine said, "Wow, I don't know what I would do. What would you do?" Her young friend said, "I'd stop pretending!"

Most of us are so enthralled with the scary tigers in our minds — our stories of loneliness, rejection, grief — that we don't realize they are in the past. They can't hurt us anymore. When we realize that the stories we are haunted by are simply that — stories

— we can be with what we actually feel directly, now, in our bodies. Tingling, pulsing, pressure, weightiness, heaviness, big black ball of concrete in the chest. And by being in immediate contact with what we feel, we see the link between feelings and what is beyond them. We see that we are so much more than any particular feeling, that, for example, when sadness is explored it may turn into a lush meadow of peace. Or that when we allow ourselves to feel the full heat of anger without expressing it, a mountain of strength and courage is revealed.

Our cat, Mookie, came to us from a friend who swore that his sweet, docile nature made him unfit to go outside. But three weeks into his kittenhood, we discovered Mookie's main purpose in life was to maim and murder. He attacked our dog, Celeste, on a daily basis — jumped on her back legs and bit into her fur — although she was ten times his size. He dangled lizards in his mouth with glee, ate goldfinches beginning with their heads and finishing off each bone, each eye, each feather. Mookie was a tyrannosaur in a cat's body. He swaggered, he destroyed, he roared. He also peed everywhere. On our bed, on Celeste's beds, on the chairs, the rugs, the couches. At first I thought he had to be sick — bladder infection, kidney disease. But the vet said his kidneys were fine, his bladder was great. This was a behavioral problem. He said, "This is a cat that wants revenge." "For what?" I asked. "For being cuddled and held and fed asparagus when most of the world is starving?"

For three years, I'd alternate between hating Mookie when he peed and loving him when he didn't. And as my friend Annie said, he made life impossible by being so impossibly gorgeous. He'd bat his light blue eyes and I'd swoon from the beauty of him. He'd turn a corner, situate himself behind a crop of violet pansies and the perfection of him — his fluffy tail, his tiny gray ears, his long whiskers — would knock me out. I've always had a bit of a problem choosing function over form. When I was twenty-eight I earned three hundred and fifty dollars every month from which to pay rent, buy food, gas, books, and go to the movies. But once I saw the little cottage on a bluff overlooking the ocean for three hundred and twenty-five dollars a month, I decided I'd rather be hungry than live anywhere else. So Mookie had his way with me because he was beautiful. "But that's the problem," another friend said. "He thinks you love him because he's beautiful. He wants to be loved for who he is. Not his looks. He's peeing to test your love."

"Gimme a break," I said.

Matt and I tried everything to stop the peeing. We got motion detectors in aerosol cans and every time he approached one of his favorite peeing spots, the container would whoosh air and scare him half to death. He learned to pee in between the whooshes. We got something called Anti-Icky Poo, which lifted the smell of cat pee from our chairs, our couch, our bed. We plugged in little units of Feliway essence that were supposed to infuse the house with a happy hormone that would make Mookie feel so good that he wouldn't want to pee. We also yelled at him, talked to him, consulted three vets about what to do.

The peeing continued. I'd get furious, kick him out of the house for an hour or two, threaten to give him away and then fall back in love. I felt like a pushover, a wimp, resolving each time that this time he peed on the chair would be the last and out he'd go. One day, he walked into my new writing room, jumped on the new couch and peed. I screamed, picked him up midstream and threw him out the door. You bastard, I thought. You ingrate. You horrible blue-eyed monster. That's it. You're leaving. He wandered back an hour later batting his iris eyes at me, but I wasn't giving in. My heart was unmeltable. I was a beauty pushover no longer.

At dinner that night, he didn't show up at the back door, even when we shook his bag of food around the yard. Besides killing, Mookie's greatest pleasure was eating. All my pets are compulsive eaters and Mookie was no exception. He'd chunk into a raw butternut squash if I left it on the counter. He'd drag a loaf of bread from the car, tear open the brown paper bag, and devour it, leaving only the crusts. He'd eat avocados, cherries, turnips. And he never missed one of his own cat food meals. Not once.

He didn't come home. Up and down the driveway we walked, shook, called, looked. No Mookie. I was convinced that I got so angry with him that he never wanted to come back. Or else that my anger provoked his anger and he was so furious that he'd stomped away. Decided to find a better home, newer places to pee.

At dawn I walked outside to look for Mookie, and as I passed a small bush outside the back door, I saw him stretched out, as if he was about to pounce on a lizard. "Mookie?" I said. But he didn't move. Heart pounding, I ran to find Matt. "Come, come, I found Mookie but something is wrong." Matt touched him. "He's cold," he said. "He's dead," he said. And we both burst into tears. Held each other. Cried for a long time. Then I said, "I killed him. My anger killed him." Matt said, "That's ridiculous. He's never missed a meal no matter how angry you've gotten at him." "Then he froze to death out here," I said. He never spent a night outside, ever. "But it's summer," Matt said. "It's not freezing outside, so how could he have frozen to death?" Through my tears I said, "It's possible, anything's possible."

We brought him to the vet's office for an autopsy. I needed to know how he died. But before the results came back, I was awash in self-blame. I yelled at him and he never came back. If only I'd let him in the house he wouldn't have died. I'm a terrible person. I'm too angry. No wonder Mookie killed things. He took after me. I remember what another vet once told me about pets: they take on diseases so that their owners can be healthy. He killed green-flecked humming-birds so I would be spared from killing other things, like my contractor, the bum. I knew my anger would destroy something someday and finally it did. And he died a terrible death. Terrible. Terrible death. Terrible person.

The next day, our vet called to say that Mookie had died of heart failure. "It looks as if he'd had congenital heart disease," he said. "He didn't freeze to death. And it wasn't a broken heart in the way you think about it," he said. "His aorta was blocked. His days were numbered from the time he was born. Think about it this way," Rob added, "he ate everything that couldn't eat him and he exacted revenge upon every living thing he encountered. For Mookie, that was a good life."

But Matt and I were in shock. It was the Death Thing all over. How could Mookie be here one day and gone the next? Where did he go? How come he wasn't fluffing his tail or biting Celeste's legs when she ran across the courtyard, which she now did quite freely since Mookie wasn't skulking behind the bird's-nest fern waiting to attack her. "The difference between someone, anyone, being physically alive and being dead is bigger than the difference between any other two opposites," my friend Katherine said. He's dead. He's gone. I couldn't grasp it. It shouldn't have happened. He was only three years old. I wanted to complain, return him to the friend who gave him to us. Get one that wasn't defective.

On the third day, as I was whipping up the self-hatred like egg whites into meringue, I remembered inquiry. Well, almost. I went to see my teacher Jeanne and *she* remembered inquiry. As I was blabbering about how horrible it was, how awful I am, she cut through the story and got to the point: "What's going on in your body?" she asked.

The first step of inquiry is to drag yourself back from wherever you are bobbing around and come back to your body. It has all the information you need.

"My body?" I asked. "Now?" I said, as if the neurons in my brain didn't have a pathway to decipher that combination of vowels and consonants.

"Yes," she said. "What is going on in your chest? Your solar plexus? What is actually there?"

Despite the habitual turning away, "now" is always better than the story about it. Always. Because there is no way to engage with, move on from or handle the to-ing and fro-ing of a story.

As soon as I lurched my attention from my-life-as-a-Barbara-Cartland-novel onto what I could sense directly, my body felt shockingly relaxed and calm. It felt as if it was made of new spring air. No occlusions. No pollution. As Jeanne asked how the clarity affected me, I noticed something I hadn't wanted to notice: that nothing was wrong. Mookie had died and nothing was wrong. My story about death and my defective personality, my criminal tendencies collided with the vividness of what I actually sensed.

As I became more and more curious about the clear space, a feeling of benevolence saturated my body, the room, the house. I understood that Mookie had lived as long as he was supposed to live. That his death had nothing to do with my value or lack of it. It wasn't a mental understanding, it was a sensate knowledge, a whole-body certainty. The brightness changed to a thick dense black, almost palpable but not sticky substance whose effect on me was stillness and peacefulness. As I sensed into the stillness, I felt boundaryless, immense. I noticed flares of sadness shooting in and out of the darkness. I was going to miss seeing Mookie's face. Feeling his presence. But that was different from ripping myself apart. Than believing that what happened shouldn't have happened or was my fault.

From self-hatred to no self. From being in hell to being at peace in twenty minutes. Talk about the opposite of bummer.

I realize that this sounds unbelievable. Impossible.

How can anyone travel from self-blame to peace at warp speed?

The ground of being is made of clarity. It's saturated with peace — which is exactly why inquiry works. When you believe your own version of events, it's like sitting in front of Niagara Falls with blinders on your eyes and earplugs in your ears — and believing that you are gazing at a wall. Just because you can't see the ongoing feast, can't feel the dynamism, can't hear the rush of water doesn't mean it's not there.

What's even more unbelievable than self-blame dissolving in peace is that we spend most of our lives wearing blinders and earplugs — and call that life. We live despairing, repetitive, stale, half-dead lives of our own making, as if that's all we can expect, and are suspicious of anyone who tells us to open our eyes and see Niagara Falls.

Another way is possible — seeing what's actually there beneath our interpretations of what's there — but it requires questioning that which most of us have never, not once, dared or even thought to question: the many assumptions we take to be truth.

This questioning is both the process and purpose of inquiry.

■ ■ ■ ■

When I am willing to question and therefore feel whatever is there — terror, hatred, anger — with curiosity, the feelings relax, because they are met with kindness and openness instead of resistance and rejection. To the degree that my feelings are familiar, that I've felt them before in similar situations — feeling left out, rejected, abandoned — the willingness to allow them offers a completely different scenario than the situations in which they first developed.

Recurrent negative feelings — those that loop in the same cycles again and again without changing — are unmet knots of our past that got frozen in time for the precise reason that they were not met with kindness or acceptance.

Can you imagine how your life would have been different if each time you were feeling sad or angry as a kid an adult said to you, "Come here, sweetheart, tell me all about it." If when you were overcome with grief at your best friend's rejection, someone said to you, "Oh darling, tell me more. Tell me where you feel those feelings. Tell me how your belly feels, your chest. I want to know every little thing. I'm here to listen to you, hold you, be with you."

All any feeling wants is be welcomed with tenderness. It wants room to unfold. It wants to relax and tell its story. It wants to dissolve like a thousand writhing snakes that with a flick of kindness become harmless strands of rope.

I tell my retreat students that they need to remember two things: to eat what they want when they're hungry and to feel what they feel when they're not. Inquiry — the feel-what-you-feel part — allows you to relate to your feelings instead of from them.

A student named Annie says, "My youngest daughter has just left for college. I wrapped my life around hers, my identity around being a mom. I can't stand the empty house. I miss her. I eat to make up for the emptiness. I feel so alone."

I ask Annie if she can tell the difference between the actual physical feeling and what she thinks she should be feeling. There is a caught-in-the-headlights look in her eyes, in the eyes of most people in the room. This is the part — feeling what they are using food to avoid — that people resist the most: they resist their weight, then they resist their feelings, and then, most of all, they resist the idea that there is gold in not resisting. That the medicine for the pain is in the pain.

She gives me a blank stare. I am certain she is thinking that her daughter's departure has already destroyed her and now I am asking her to actually feel the destruction more.

"No way," she says, "I will fall apart if I do that."

"That's a story," I say, "and I understand why you have it. But tell me if you actually sense the aloneness in your body. Tell me if it has a color. Tell me if it has a shape. Tell me if there is tingling or vibrating or pulsing when you feel alone."

She closes her eyes. She says, "It is black. It is so thick that it feels like it will eat everything that comes into contact with it. It will make everything disappear."

I ask her how the blackness affects her when she actually lets herself sense it. "Blackness," I say, "just deep blackness without any reaction to it, without any story about it, without any ideas about it."

"Well," she says, "when I feel the blackness itself, it just feels like space. It feels quiet and deep and peaceful like floating in space unobstructed. No gravity. Free."

Then she starts to cry. "I don't want to be out there alone," she says. "I don't want to be floating by myself."

I ask her what is so terrible about quiet,

peaceful blackness.

She says, "My mother left me alone with my uncle. Over and over and over again. He was grimy and slimy and smelled like alcohol. One time he put his hands on my breast but I bit his finger. When I told my mother what he did, she said I imagined it. She said he was her brother and wouldn't do anything like that. I hated being left alone with him. She didn't believe me. I felt like I was alone in the universe. The adults were crazy. They hurt people, they lied. It was just me."

This is the hard part for anyone, for me. To see that the associations we have with feelings are in the past. To see that we avoid feelings because of the story we tell ourselves about them. Grief hurts, sadness hurts, but it's not the feelings that destroy us. It's what we tell ourselves about the feelings. It's that we perceive a present-day feeling through historical eyes. Through the eyes of a child.

Since I know Annie well, I also know she has worked with the abuse for many years in therapy. The feelings about it are no longer new or fresh, but understanding the association between aloneness and the abuse is. To allow herself full reign of her own life, of her own power, of her own presence, she needs to see the link she has created between loneliness in the past and aloneness in the present. Only then will she be able to see that she is spending the present fearing what's passed.

When you inquire, you begin with whatever is happening now — from wanting to eat an entire pizza to wanting to crawl into bed and stay there for the next fifty years. You don't assume that you know what you need to do or where you need to go. You become curious about feelings and sensations. You listen to your body. You stop bossing yourself around.

Any inquiry starts with wanting to know something you don't know. If you think you already know what's wrong and how to fix it, there's no need to inquire. Wanting to know something you don't know activates your curiosity; it elicits your openness. It evokes the part of you that is not a conglomeration of old beliefs, ideas, self-images, stories, identifications. The ground of your being that is already saturated with peace, clarity, compassion — the Niagara Falls part.

Inquiry is body based; it is not a mental process. You sense what it feels like to be inside your skin, your arms, your legs. You notice the sensation and you notice the location of the sensation. Sensation, location, sensation, location. If, for instance, you are feeling sad, you ask yourself where that feeling is located in your body. You notice a gray heap of ashes in your chest, and up pops the belief that "love exists for other people but not for me." You become curious about that belief. How old were you when you first learned that? And what were your feelings at the time that never got noticed or felt or understood?

Sometimes when I ask students what they are feeling in their bodies, they have no idea. It's been a couple of light-years since they felt anything in or about their bodies that wasn't judgment or loathing. So it's good to ask some questions that allow you to focus on the sensations themselves. You can ask yourself if the feeling has a shape, a temperature, a color. You can ask yourself how it affects you to feel this. And since no feeling is static, you keep noticing the changes that occur in your body as you ask yourself these questions.

If you get stuck, it's usually because you're having a reaction to a particular feeling — you don't want to feel this way, you'd rather be happy right now, you don't like people who feel like this — or you're locked into comparing/judging mode.

About reactions: feelings are in the body, reactions are in the head; a reaction is the mental deduction of a feeling. (And beliefs are reactions that we've had so many times that we believe they are true.) In an attempt not to feel what is uncomfortable, the mind will often rant and ramble and tell us how awful it all is.

Here is some of what you may hear: *This pain will never end. The sadness will overwhelm me. If I let myself feel it, I will not be able to function.* Once you know that these kinds of reactions will come up, you can notice them and keep inquiring.

Be precise. "I feel a gray heap of ashes in my chest" rather than "I feel something odd and heavy." Don't try to direct the process by having preferences or agendas. Let the inquiry move in its own direction. Notice whatever arises, even if it surprises you. "Oh, I thought I was sad, but now I see that this is loneliness. It feels like a ball of rubber bands in my stomach." Welcome the rubber bands. Give them room. Watch what happens.

Keep coming back to the direct sensations in your body. Pay attention to things you've never told anyone, secrets you've kept to yourself. Do not censor anything. Do not get discouraged. It takes awhile to trust the immediacy of inquiry since we are so used to directing everything with our minds. It is helpful, though not necessary, to do inquiry with a guide or a partner so that you can have a witness and a living reminder to come back to the sensation and the location.

Most of all, remember that inquiry is not about discovering answers to puzzling problems but a direct and experiential revelation process. It's fueled by love. And wanting to know who you are when you are not being run by your past. It's like taking a dive into the secret of existence itself; it is full of surprises, twists, side trips. You engage in it because you want to penetrate the unknown, comprehend the incomprehensible. Because when you evoke curiosity and openness with a lack of judgment, you align yourself with beauty and delight and love — for their own sake. You become the benevolence of God in action.

# CHAPTER EIGHT:
## MARRIED TO
## AMAZEMENT

I first heard about meditation in the early seventies from a guy named David who was a student of a little guru with a lot of money. David and his fellow meditators lived together in a house in New York where they practiced celibacy and meditation; the first, according to the little guru, being a prerequisite of the other. David explained that meditation was like being lifted on currents of warm air. Like a hawk soaring in lazy circles. "Your mind gets very quiet," he said, "and something else — something sweet and glowing and holy — takes over." I was all ready to sign up when David's arm soared around my neck and grabbed my breast in a holy sort of way. I removed his hand and told him to get lost.

A few months later, I found myself in India, where I learned mantra meditation: saying a phrase over and over to quiet the mind. But the phrase — "So-ham," which

means "I am that" (which is eternal, unconditioned, beyond time and space) — was in
Sanskrit and sounded very much like "Ho-
hum" and no matter how many times I said
it, I'd fall asleep.

Since then, I've tried dozens of different
meditations: streaming light meditations,
visualization meditations, multisyllabic
mantra meditations. I've tried Tibetan Buddhist meditations, Sufi meditations, Taoist
nonmeditation meditations. And while none
of them did what I thought they were going
to do — turn my mind into an ocean of bliss
— I am nonetheless exhorting you to meditate.

Here's a tiny snapshot of why.

Last night I went to bed rather cheerfully.
Matt had just returned from a weeklong
work trip, twelve double Bowl of Beauty
peonies were blooming in my garden, and
I'd had a productive writing day. Also, the
earth had survived yet another twenty-four
hours without a nuclear blast. Life was
good.

Then came the middle of the night. My
mind, which had been in repose during the
previous eighty-six times I'd woken up,
started playing its familiar music. And these,
more or less, are the tunes:

Joe (our contractor who had installed a leaky roof) still hasn't returned my call. I bet he's not intending to. I'm going to have to call a lawyer, but it's probably going to cost so much to pay the damned lawyer that by the time I get done forking out the cash for those bills, I could have gotten a new roof. That fucking contractor. I need to call the lawyer first thing in the morning. My throat hurts. I wonder what the signs of esophageal cancer are? Is my computer on? Maybe I should go look up the signs of throat cancer. I'm getting old. Soon I'm going to die — and since Matt will die first, I'll be alone. Men always leave first. Why didn't we have children? I know people say that having children so that you will have someone to take care of you when you are old and no one else cares is not a good reason, but what were they thinking when they said that? Maybe it's not too late to adopt. We could go to Russia, maybe even the town where our grand-parents came from. If we knew which or where it was. Latvia? Litvia? Minsk? Are those even real words? We'd have to spend months there. At least we could drink vodka, but first I'd have to like the taste of it. It's late, I need to go back to sleep. I think I'll get a glass of water.

Water. California had its driest spring in 156 years. Soon there won't be any water. The earth is either going to be scorched or under water. And we're definitely living in the scorched part. Oh man. I better learn to eat roots and tree stumps and leaves, starting tomorrow. Because what if Matt dies and I am old and alone and haven't learned to eat stumps yet? I'm going to google adopting in Russia first thing in the morning. After I call the contractor. Or maybe the lawyer.

These are the ravings of a paranoid, frightened, bitter person. Someone you wouldn't want your children to be alone with. And this was a good night.

After decades of meditating, my mind, left to its default position, does not soar like a hawk. And for the first ten years of my practice I was bitterly disappointed by my shocking lack of progress. I thought I was meditating to smooth out the rough edges, to transform my anger, to, uh, become a different person. Someone like the Meryl Streep character in *Defending Your Life* who ran into burning buildings to save sick people and children. But it turns out that it's hopeless. The mind, as Catherine Ingram says, is mad. And this is very good news. Because once you accept the madness, once you stop trying to reform what cannot be reformed, you can pay attention to what isn't mad. Which, in my opinion, is one of the main purposes of meditation.

Last night, for example, as I was finding fault with the immediate universe, there was a tiny voice that understood that my mind was playing its usual songs and I didn't need to listen. I've heard the tunes before; they usually fall into the "They Did Me Wrong" mix or the "I Did Them Wrong" mix or "A Major Catastrophe Is Imminent" mix. (The "Dying Alone" refrain is also a favorite, but that falls into the "Catastrophe" medley as a subset of "Personal Catastrophe.")

A woman in my retreat said, "Why on earth would anyone want to meditate? Why would I want to sit quietly when there is so much to do — and so much that is infinitely more compelling?" Another woman said, "My mind is the most interesting thing about me. My mind is what makes me different from other people. My mind is what helped me graduate from Harvard Law with honors. Why would I want to pay attention to anything besides my very smart mind?"

And the answer is: Minds are useful when we need to conceptualize, plan, theorize. But when we depend on them to guide our inner lives, we're lost. Minds are excellent at presenting a thousand different variations of the past and conjuring them into a future. And then scaring us with most of them.

Most of the time we don't question our minds. We believe in their lunacy. We have a thought — my contractor is never going to call me back — that evokes a corresponding emotion (anger, anxiety, blame) and we are suddenly on the phone with the lawyer, convinced that we hired a thief who is now on his way to Costa Rica with our money. The louse.

Or we pass by a bakery window and see a bear claw and we are suddenly convinced we have to have it now. Convinced that we were born to be standing here, at this very window, about to walk into the bakery and get it, eat it. Be transported to a bliss realm. Meditation develops the capacity to question your mind. Without it, you are at the mercy of every thought, every desire, every wave of emotion. You become unhinged, dependent on whether things are going well that day or not. Whether anyone has rejected you that day or not. If nothing kicks up the "They Did Me Wrong" mix, or the "I Am Fat and Unloved and Will Always Be This Way" mix you might have a good eating day. But if you pass a mirror and don't like what you see, if you have a fight with friend, a partner, a boss, a child, there is nowhere to go but your mind, which usually means listening to one of the familiar whipped-up melodies. And believing every word of it.

When you spend time watching the mind, you notice the familiar medleys and you notice what is noticing the medleys — the stillness that is apart from them. After a while, the stillness feels more like you than the top ten medleys. You begin to love that which is not caught up in the hysteria. Love the stillness. Love the spaciousness. Love the peace. Meditation helps you discover what you love that you didn't know you loved because you were so caught up in your mind that you didn't realize there was anything else there. The value of meditation is that it helps you first discover — and then bring yourself back to — what you love.

In her poem "When Death Comes," Mary Oliver writes: "When it's over, I want to say: all my life / I was a bride married to amazement."

Me, too. I want a life of amazement. I want to show up for what Zorba the Greek called "the whole catastrophe." And after living through decades of being married to obsession and self-constructed suffering, I have found that being married to amazement means showing up in the only place from which to experience it: here, now, in this very moment.

Usually, when people hear the word meditation, they think of transcending this clunky earthly plane. The kind of meditation I refer to has nothing to do with transcending or leaving or changing yourself in any way — and everything to do with its opposite: showing up where you already are.

In my retreats, I teach a simple meditation that uses the breath as an anchor — which makes anyone who lives aboveground eligible. We use concentration to help you become aware of the place between the top of your pubic bone and the bottom of the sternum: your belly.

Uh-oh.

Just the word is enough to send some of us — I won't mention names — screaming from the room. We hate the area "down there" — and, paradoxically, that is why we often feel so crazed. The belly is located in the center of our bodies and is in fact the center of our grounding. (Eastern mystics believe the belly is the center of our spirit and that our souls reside there.) Sensing it from the inside — whether it's pulsing or tingling or vibrating, whether it's warm or cold or numb — helps us become undeniably and viscerally aware we are alive. We sense the actual physical presence of our life force (by sensing our belly).

When you ignore your belly, you become homeless. You spend your life trying to erase your own existence. Apologizing for yourself. Feeling like a ghost. Eating to take up space, eating to give yourself the feeling that you have weight here, you belong here, you are allowed to be yourself — but never quite believing it because you don't sense yourself directly.

During an exercise I taught at a retreat, the need for the belly meditation became very apparent. I gave each student five feet of red string and asked them to make a circle around their bodies — and to sit in the middle of the circle they had constructed. I said, "This is your spot. Your space. Make the circle as big or as little as you want, but as soon as you close both ends of the string, imagine that your energy extends from your center to the edge of the circle."

Easy instructions, elementary exercise. At least five people started crying as soon as they made their circle. "I've never felt that it was okay to take my own place," someone said. "I can't make the circle big enough," someone else replied. "I've crushed myself into such a tiny corner of my body for thirty years that I feel as if I need a whole room now. Do you have more string? Can I move into the hall?" Another person couldn't bring the string in close enough to her body. "I don't feel as if I'm supposed to have a body," she said. "Taking up space here is wrong."

My students are mothers, teachers, doctors, actors, psychiatrists, psychologists, attorneys, college students, midwives, housewives, inventors, CEOs. They are no more or less neurotic than the rest of us. And yet. A piece of red string from Walgreens made it graphically apparent that they were not living at the center of their own lives. That they didn't feel allowed.

After that, I started teaching a simple belly meditation in which I asked people to become aware of sensations in their belly (numbness and emptiness count as sensations). Every time their mind wandered — even when they found themselves in the middle of a paragraph or deep in the throes of a mind medley — I asked them to begin counting their breaths so they could anchor their concentration. Starting with the number one and saying it on the out breath, they'd count to seven and begin again. If they were able to stay concentrated on the sensations in their belly centers, they didn't need to use counting as a concentration anchor.

After teaching this meditation for only five days, I found that people said things like

"Oh. My. God. I feel like I've been waiting for this belly thing my whole life. Waiting for myself to arrive."

"If you had told me we were going to focus on the belly before I got here, I wouldn't have come."

"I feel like my belly is the size of Arkansas, and so the last thing I wanted to do was climb inside of it. But I am amazed at what happened. For the first time in my forty-two years, I actually feel like it's me here, living this life."

"I'm actually here living instead of pretending to live while I am waiting to die."

"I realize now that I have a right to be here. I am not sure what I've been doing all these years, but it hasn't been this."

For some people a twenty-minute meditation will consist of finding themselves in the middle of a familiar refrain and bringing themselves back to their breath. Nine hundred times. For some people, a twenty-minute meditation will consist of being lost in one long story only to remember (and only at the sound of the bell that marks the end of the twenty minutes) that they have forgotten their breath for the duration. Some people are better able to concentrate than others. Some people are actually able to feel sensations like pulsing or tingling or fluttering in their bellies. It doesn't matter. What matters is that you begin the process of bringing yourself back to your body, to your belly, to your breath because they — and not the mind medleys — are here now. And it is only here, only now that you can make a decision to eat or not eat. To occupy your own body or to vacate your arms and your legs while still breathing and go through your days as a walking head.

Owning your own presence — the direct, sensate, immediate experience of being in your body — by grounding yourself in your belly has everything to do with compulsive eating. By definition, eating compulsively is eating without regard to the body's cues; it therefore follows that when you develop the capacity to steer your attention back to your body, are aware of what it says and are willing to listen to it, compulsion falls away.

Meditation is a tool to shake yourself awake. A way to discover what you love. A practice to return yourself to your body when the mind medleys threaten to usurp your sanity.

But. That doesn't necessarily translate to being unequivocally cheerful about it. Some days, for instance, I wake up in a chirpy sort of mood. I want to start writing immediately or speak to a friend. But since I have a daily practice of meditating before eating, writing, drinking chai, or talking on the phone, I feel caught. The thought of sitting down by myself in silence for half an hour seems like getting my gums scraped. I procrastinate. I take an hour to do the breakfast dishes, locate an emergency somewhere to which I need to attend. On those days, I'm usually equating meditation with a need to get somewhere special by being someone who meditates. And sometimes I believe my self-made decree and rebel. I don't sit. But most of the time I sit quietly anyway, and the second I get myself in my seat, the second I start being aware of the breath and the belly, there is an abrupt shift. The world of time I'd been inhabiting drops away. Everything I was rushing to do dissolves. Sounds become louder. Sensations become stronger. Squawking birds, raspy breath, howling wind. Warm dog breath, creaking door, ringing phone. Pulsing belly. Tingling hands. And even that's beyond what it feels like because what it feels like is that there is no difference between outside and inside. Suddenly all the goodness everywhere is here. In the space that used to be me is amazement married to itself. Which is why I still meditate every day and recommend that you do the same.

# CHAPTER NINE:
## BREATH BY BREATH

"Mr. Duffy lived a short distance from his body." I wish that was my line (but alas, it belongs to James Joyce), since it perfectly expresses the mass twenty-first-century evacuation from our bodies. We think of ourselves as walking heads with bothersome, unattractive appendages attached. It's as if we'd rather pretend we don't have bodies. As if they are the source of our trouble, and if only we could get rid of or otherwise dismiss them, we'd be fine. We crash around in our arms and legs, let them lift for us, hold our children for us, walk for us without ever taking time to actually live in them. Until we are about to lose them.

An article in *The New Yorker* about people who romanticize committing suicide (the ultimate body-removal technique) by jumping off the Golden Gate Bridge quoted one man, saying, "I instantly realized that everything in my life that I'd thought was unfixable was totally fixable — except for having just jumped."

Sigh.

The problem isn't that we have bodies; the problem is that we're not living in them.

When I first talk to retreat students about inhabiting their bodies, their eyes glaze over; the air suddenly feels as if it's made of lead. The body is so — well — unglamorous. This is not what they came for. They want to learn how to have different bodies, not occupy the ones they have now.

One of my students was convinced that her ample forty-year-old, mother-of-three-children thighs were the source of her suffering. After spending years obsessing about each new wrinkle of cellulite — how she looked in jeans, how her life could be different with different thighs — she woke up in excruciating pain after a liposuction operation. She remembers the recovery, more painful than she ever imagined. Remembers looking down on her thighs a thousand times over the next few months to assess their newfound smoothness. A year later, upon coming to her first retreat, she said, "It is devastating to realize that I paid all that money and no one, not my husband or my sister or me — can tell the difference between my thighs now and my thighs then.

They don't seem to care, no less notice, that my thighs have less cellulite. I didn't want to go through life hating my thighs and now we've spent half our savings on the operation and I still can't stand my thighs."

I tell her that I have never met anyone for whom years of rejection and hatred suddenly and miraculously turned to love, even after a face-lift, LAP-BAND surgery, liposuction. When you love something you wish it goodness; when you hate something, you wish to annihilate it. Change happens not by hatred but by love. Change happens when you understand what you want to change so deeply that there is no reason to do anything but act in your own best interest. When you begin to inhabit your body from the inside, when you stop looking at it through, as my friend Mary Jane Ryan says, "bank camera eyes," any other option except taking care of it is unthinkable.

No matter how much you loathe yourself or believe life would be better if your thighs were thinner or your hips were narrower or your eyes were wider apart, your essence — that which makes you you — needs the body to articulate its vision, its needs, its love. Inhaling your child's baby-powder-neck perfume requires flesh, nose, senses.

Presence, enlightenment, insight are only possible because there is a body in which they unfold. In *The Lovely Bones* by Alice Sebold, when the murdered narrator, Susie, wants to kiss her boyfriend, she slips into her friend's body to feel the warmth of lips on lips — as if having a body was heaven itself.

Despite your argument with your physicality, the fact is that you are here and the 151,000 people who have died today are not. I heard a meditation years ago in which a teacher suggested that we think about what people who had recently died would give to be sitting where we were. To be sitting in any body, in any room. He said, "Think of what they would give to have just one more moment inside this physical form, these arms, these legs, this beating heart and no other." I gathered that the dead to whom he referred didn't really care about the size of anyone's thighs.

Your body is the piece of the universe you've been given; as long as you have a pulse, it presents you with an ongoing shower of immediate sensate experiences. Red, salt, loneliness, heat. When a friend says something painful to you, your chest aches. When you fall in love, that same chest feels like fireworks and waterfalls and explosions of ecstasy. When you are lonely, your body feels empty. When you are sad, it feels as if there is a Mack truck sitting on your lungs. Grief feels like tidal waves knocking you down, joy like champagne bubbles welling up in your arms, your legs, your belly. Our minds are like politicians; they make stuff up, they twist the truth. Our minds are masters at blame, but our bodies . . . our bodies don't lie. Which is, of course, why so many of us learned to zip out of them at the first sign of trouble.

The ability to live a short distance from our bodies was, at one time, our best chance at survival. Since children experience emotional pain in and through their bodies, and since there were no resources for releasing that pain, we became skilled at getting out of Dodge — bolting — in a hurry. In developing the skill to leave our bodies, we avoided being destroyed by the onslaught of potentially fragmenting pain. It was a lifesaving exit.

But the fast track up and out of physicality has become maladaptive for two main reasons: it truncates our ability to feel and therefore to move through the situations that arise in our lives. When we are bowled over by grief and our response is to eat a pizza, we halt our ability to move through the grief as well as our confidence that it won't destroy us. If you don't allow a feeling to begin, you also don't let it end.

The second reason that living a short distance from the body is maladaptive is that since the body is the only place in which to experience hunger and fullness, any attempts at ending compulsive eating are doomed to fail. When you start eating without first being aware of whether or not your body is hungry, the only signal telling you to put down your fork is nauseating discomfort.

I realize that coming home to your body after a lifetime of being at war with it might not seem appealing, especially if it is uncomfortable to sit or walk within its confines. But just because homecomings are rocky does not mean you should spend the rest of your life avoiding them.

Reminding yourself that you have a body during any given day looks like this: You are lurching along and suddenly catch yourself walking without realizing you are walking. Then you remember to be aware of your breath — your abdomen moving, your lungs filling with air. You sense some kind of flow or density or warmth or tingling in your legs. You notice that you have arms, that you have hands, and that one of them is now lifting a pen or a child. You arrive in your body for a moment and you are gone again, floating from place to place with no clear remembrance of the transition. Then you suddenly land here again — first one breath, then another — and it's as if everything is new. You feel your child's breath on your face. You hear the scratch of the pen on the paper. You fall into the sound as if it is the first note of a symphony. The next moment you are catapulted into seeing without seeing, hearing without hearing.

You bring yourself back to your body about a thousand times a day. Even if you live in an urban environment with wailing sirens and blaring car horns, you can still focus on physical sensations — the contact your legs are making with the chair, the sound of the computer keys hitting the board, the slight chill in the air. In this way, it becomes possible to live, as writer John Tarrant says, "in our true range, and not go around missing things, as if we knew countries only from their airports and hotels."

Thich Nhat Hanh, the Vietnamese Buddhist teacher, says, "There is no way to happiness — happiness is the way." Just so, there is no way back to the body; the body is the way. You leave and then you return. Leave and return. You forget and then you remember. Forget. Remember. One breath and then another. One step and then another. It's that simple. And it doesn't matter how long you've been gone; what matters is that you've returned. With each return, each sound, each felt sensation, there is relaxation, recognition, and gratitude. Gratitude begets itself, ripens into flowers, snow falls, mountains of more gratitude. Soon you begin wondering where you've been all this time. How you wandered so far. And you realize that torture isn't having these arms or these legs; it's being so convinced that God is out there, in another place, another realm that you miss the lavender slip of moon, your own awakened presence.

# Chapter Ten:
# The GPS from
# the Twilight Zone

The biggest obstacle to any kind of transformation is the voice that tells you it's impossible. It says: *You've always been like this, you'll always be like this, what's the point. No one ever really changes. Might as well eat. By the way, have you taken a look at your arms recently? And what were you thinking when you wore those pants today? Have you noticed the rolls cascading over your pants? And excuse me, did you forget to put on makeup today or is that what you look like when it's already on? That hair. Those thighs. Why do you even bother? Did you just say what I think you said to your boss? Who are you, Queen of the Universe? How many times do you have to fall flat on your face before you learn to keep your mouth shut?*

Anne Lamott calls it Radio Station KFKD. Less lyrical people (like Sigmund Freud) call it the superego, the internalized parent, the inner critic. I call it The Voice.

Everyone has The Voice. It's a developmental necessity. You need to learn not to put your hands in fire, walk into oncoming traffic, stick electrical wires into water. You need to learn that you probably won't be welcomed into other people's houses if you throw food on their walls or put snakes in their beds. When external authority figures such as parents, teachers or family members communicate verbal and nonverbal instructions about physical and emotional survival, we coalesce those voices into one voice — The Voice — by a process called introjection (internalizing authority figures).

According to developmental psychologists, The Voice is fully operative in most of us by the time we are four years old, after which it functions as a moral compass, a deterrent to questionable behavior. Instead of being afraid of the disapproval of our parents, we become afraid of the disapproval of The Voice. Instead of being punished for daring to disagree with our mothers or fathers, we adults punish ourselves for daring to believe that our lives could be different. We become risk aversive. Frightened of change.

The Voice steps in when we want to challenge the status quo. When we want to do anything our parents wouldn't have wanted us to do. Depending on our particular parents, this could mean anything from traveling to Asia (All that icky malaria. Dysentery. Leprosy. Better stay home) to trusting our own instincts (Trust your instincts? Hello? Have you noticed where that has gotten you?) to using your relationship with food as a doorway to your true nature (I'll show you your true nature. It looks like you snarfing down those potato chips last week).

Some people — I, for instance — are slow to internalize The Voice. When I was eight years old, my friend Amanda and I sat on a stoop on a languid summer New York afternoon and watched people walk by. We were fascinated by their butts, enthralled by each melon-shaped protrusion. Unable to restrain ourselves any longer, we roused ourselves from our torpor and devised a game: one of us would tiptoe very slowly behind a stranger as they sashayed down the street. In the ripest of all moments, we would pinch their butt and tear down the street in the other direction. Our game worked well for about a half hour until Amanda pinched Ethel and Harry Sherman's son Martin's butt, after which Martin told Ethel and Ethel called my mother, who walked outside and caught me pinching the butt of Murray Wise, her dentist. Big Trouble. "What makes you think it's okay to go around pinching people's rear ends," my mother shrieked at Amanda and me as she apologized profusely to Dr. Wise. "It's fun," we chimed together. "It's a violation — big word, look it up in the dictionary — of their privacy," my mother said. "You need to stop this right now! Now! Not tomorrow, not next week, now! Get back in the house immediately."

The Voice controls the impulses, mediates between the proper and the outrageous; one of its primary functions is to suppress behavior that could lead to one's arrest. In hooligans like me, this process takes longer than usual.

Within the first two hours of the beginning of a retreat, I ask my students to make a list of ten criticisms they've made about themselves since they walked in the door. Just ten? someone usually asks. How about a hundred? Five hundred?

Then I ask a few of them to read the lists out loud in the tone of their Voice. The particulars change from person to person. They vary from: *I can't believe I came to another thing on weight* to *What is WRONG with me for thinking I could wear a sleeveless dress* to *My toenails are disgusting* to *I am wasting my time and I should go home now.* Sometimes The Voice says, *You're trying too hard.* Sometimes it says, *You're not trying hard enough.* But its main message is always the same: *Your impulses cannot be trusted. Listen only to me. Depend on me. Otherwise you'll die a failure. You idiot.*

Sound extreme? It is. Sound like you wouldn't let anyone talk to you like that ever? Perhaps. But you talk to yourself like that from the time you awaken until you close your eyes at night without one teeny thought about the cruelty factor; you've become inured to the insults. And therein lies the pickle: The Voice feels and sounds so much like you that you believe it *is* you. You think you are telling yourself the truth. And you are utterly convinced that without The Voice as your conscience, your wild and unruly tendencies would run amok.

Let's take an example that probably occurs with alarming frequency, possibly many times a day. You are humming along with your morning routine when you try on an old pair of pants. Uh-oh. You can't get your right leg into the designated hole. The hole that just last year was already a size bigger than the year before. The Voice says, *Look at*

161

*you! You are pathetic! Your thighs are the size of the Rocky Mountains.* You look down at the appendages in question. Hmm, you think, my thighs really are taking over my body, the living room, the neighborhood. The Voice says, *You should be ashamed of yourself!* You agree. You think, I *am* ashamed of myself, look how I've let myself go. The Voice says, *Bad bad bad.* You think, Bad thighs. Bad me.

A few minutes later you notice that you feel as if you've been vaporized. In the space that you once occupied there is a ghostly dread and a vague feeling of being needy, weak and fat. Within minutes, you've ricocheted into feeling as if your life is not worth anything.

Yet.

Nothing — not one thing — has changed since earlier this morning when you felt spunky, feisty, irreverent. The objective fact is that you can't fit into your pants. The reality is that you've gained weight in the last few months. But why should gaining weight have the power to devastate every last shred of your well-being? Why can't you realize you've gained weight and make some decisions about how to proceed with some degree of wisdom and self-worth?

Because the intention of The Voice is to

stun you, not activate your intelligence or equanimity. In its early development, it was biologically adaptive: it kept you from being rejected by those you depend on. Now it is archaic, a vestigial remnant from childhood that, despite its ersatz usefulness, is now running your life and rendering you incapable of acting with true discernment and intelligence. Its main warning is: *Don't cross the line. Maintain the status quo.*

The Voice usurps your strength, passion and energy — and turns them against you. Its unique way of blending objective truth — that you've gained weight — with moral judgment — that therefore you are a complete loser — leaves you feeling defeated and weak, which then leaves you susceptible to latching on to the next quick fix or miracle cure. Anything to stop feeling so desperate.

The Voice is merciless, ravaging, life destroying. The Voice makes you feel so weak, so paralyzed, so incompetent that you wouldn't dare question (its) authority. Its intent is to keep you from being thrown out of whatever it perceives as the circle of love.

Some of my students are convinced that The Voice is an exact replica of their mothers or their fathers and that nothing short of an exorcism will rid themselves of its harangues. And while The Voice may sound suspiciously like either one or both of our parental units, it's good to remember that it usually is a composite of authority figures with particular emphasis on the primary caretakers.

In my family, my mother had the market cornered on lung capacity and vocal displays. She'd say things like, "You do that one more time and I'm going to send you flying into the middle of next week!" And "Bored? You say you're bored? Go bang your head against the wall, and when you stop you'll feel better." When these statements were combined with concomitant hand gestures and eye bulges, they produced their intended results: I skulked away feeling like my existence was a bad mistake. Also, that questioning her actions led to disastrous consequences.

My version of The Voice has the same inflections, the same sarcasm, the same singsongy way of putting me down as my mother did. But its content also includes the Laws of Living According to Bernie Roth, my father, who, when I was trying to write my first book, said, "I heard that someone recently submitted an unsigned manuscript of Charles Dickens to a publisher and the book was rejected! What makes you think you're a better writer than Dickens?" The first time he heard me speak in front of a large audience, my father said, "You have charisma. Hitler did, too." This from a man whose family of thirty-three was gassed at Auschwitz. And just like my mother's screaming at me did, my father's quiet measured statements left me feeling cut down, defeated, incapable.

I tell these stories not to blame my parents (word on the street is that I unintention-ingly accomplished that task in my other books. Recently, my mother and stepfather were at a health fair where my stepfather was selling Xango, a miracle rain forest drink. A nutritionist was deep in conversa-tion with Dick when he asked if she'd read my books. "Yes," she said, "I use them all the time." Dick said, "I'm her stepfather." He turned to my mother and said, "This is her mother." The nutritionist glared. Finally she said to my mother, "You know." Pause. Beat. Silence. "Geneen had a miserable childhood!" and she stalked away. My mother called after her, "Yes, I know. I was there!"). At this point, thirty-seven years after I left their house, it's not about either one of my parents (a fact I find somewhat inconvenient since blame is so, well, cleansing) but about my awareness of how they are installed in me.

Even if you were one of the lucky ones and had parents who were kind and loving and attuned to your every expression, you would still have The Voice installed in your psyche — and that voice would still need to be challenged. Because even the most attuned parents see their children through biased lenses. They pass on their own definitions of success and spirituality, love and creativity, which are inevitably out of sync with their child's unique needs.

Children are tropistic; they grow in the direction of light and attention. That which is ignored in childhood does not develop. If a child is valued for her accomplishments, she will learn to value what she does more than who she is — and The Voice will step in when she is not fulfilling its accomplishment quota. If your parents were unaware of that which couldn't be accomplished or seen or proved, you grew up ignoring those dimensions of yourself. And The Voice will step in as cynicism and doubt when you veer into the world beyond appearances.

The Voice saps you of strength, cuts you off at the knees, and positions you in a world modeled on past authority figures who bark directions that are often cruel and almost always irrelevant to who you are and what you love. By co-opting your clarity and objective knowing, The Voice renders you incapable of contacting your own authority. It treats you as a child in need of a moral compass, but its due north does not include any terrain that is fresh or new. Think of The Voice as a Global Positioning System from the twilight zone. When you follow its directions, you spend your life trying to find streets that no longer exist in a city that vanished decades ago. Then you wonder why you feel so unbearably lost.

Byron Katie says, "I love my thoughts. I'm just not tempted to believe them." The moment you stop believing The Voice, the moment you hear the *You are the worst person in the world. You are selfish and shallow with a dry withered heart and elephant skin neck,* and you say, "Uh-huh, right, so what else is new?" or "Really? I am the worst person in the world? Is that true?" or "Honey, sounds like you need a couple dozen margaritas. Talk to me after you've had them," you are free. Freedom is hearing The Voice ramble and posture and lecture and not believing a word of it.

When you disengage from The Voice, you have access to yourself and everything The Voice supposedly offers: clarity and intelligence and true discernment. Strength and value and joy. Compassion. Curiosity. Love. Nothing is wrong because there is no right with which to compare it. When you stop responding to the continual comments on your thighs, your value, your very existence, when you no longer believe that anyone, especially The Voice, knows what's supposed to be happening, simple facts remain. Breath. Air. Skin touching chair. Hand on glass. Waistband digging into flesh. When you release yourself — even one time — from The Voice, you suddenly realize how long you've been mistaking its death grip for your life. You're Ingrid Betancourt, free after years of being chained by your captor.

Then.

You can ask yourself if you are comfortable at this weight. If you feel healthy, energetic, awake. And if the answer is no, you can ask yourself what you could do about it that would fit your day-to-day life. What you can live with, what you can maintain. What stirs your heart. I often tell people in my retreats that unless there is a resounding Yes when they hear me speak, unless they long for the kind of engagement in their own process that I describe, they need to find another way of cracking the code of their relationship with food so that they are no longer standing outside themselves trying desperately to get in. Listening to and engaging in the antics of The Voice keeps you outside yourself. It keeps you bound. Keeps you ashamed, anxious, panicked. No real or long-lasting change will occur as long as you are kneeling at the altar of The Voice.

Despite writing down their self-criticisms during the first day of the retreat, despite naming The Voice's presence, almost every student gets reentranced by it over the next day or two. Since The Voice feels so much like you, and since you are utterly convinced that without it you would romp through your life without restraint or morality, releasing yourself from its grip takes a bit of time; it happens in stages.

You begin by naming The Voice and its effect on you. And while that sounds like an easy task, it is more like pulling steel away from a magnet. Often you are not aware that you are under the influence until you are reeling from its harangues. You notice that you felt like yourself ten minutes ago, but now you feel like Superman after he's been exposed to Kryptonite by Lex Luthor: disappeared, diminished, weak, incapable, humiliated, ashamed.

The biggest challenge at the naming-and-disengaging-stage is that since you believe everything The Voice has said, you also believe that you need to hide your defects from other people lest they withdraw in abject horror. You believe that The Voice knows the truth and you don't want anyone else to discover how monstrous you are. How dark. How unredeemable. Hiding seems like an act of self-preservation. It seems like your only option if you want to have any kindness or love in your life. When you are in total agreement with The Voice, you convince yourself that your best and only recourse is to be ashamed of yourself and to try harder to get it right. Be The Voice's idea of you. Be someone different, someone you're not.

This is when every moment that you've ever spent (when you weren't under the influence) paying attention to your own being, to the invisible world, to watching your mind — every moment you've spent dropping the coins of your attention into the well of mindfulness — returns to you now as the awareness that *this collapsed place is not you.* Although it feels familiar and although it feels like tar baby — the more you thrash the stucker you get — it is not you. You know this because you've already experienced moment upon moment of delight, of peace, of being happy for no reason. You already know yourself to be that which cannot be named or attacked or destroyed. And that awareness functions now to separate you from what is not you. From your story about how unredeemable you are. From your shame at being the stale, rehashed, familiar story of yourself. And because you've come to love life without the story, you without your past, you are less and less willing to endure the suffering of merging with The Voice. You begin to prefer simplicity over complication. Freedom over familiarity.

I tell those who haven't experienced themselves without The Voice that they need to live as if. Live as if they know that they are worth their own time. Live as if they deserve to take care of their bodies. Live as if the possibilities they long for actually exist. Living as if creates a bridge to a new way of living. It allows you to see that something else is possible. That you really can walk, talk, eat as if you deserve to be here.

My retreat assistant Loren says that when she was first learning to disengage from The Voice, she needed to speak to it in ways she was not allowed to speak to her parents.

She had to say things like "FUCK YOU! Go away! Go pick on someone your own size." Since anger was not allowed in her family, and since The Voice seemed to mimic her parents, it was both shocking and liberating to tell The Voice to fuck off. In the moment after she mustered up the courage to defend herself from the cruelty of The Voice, there was relief, freedom and a sense that she, Loren, was occupying her body again instead of being controlled by a Darth Vader clone.

Once you name what has happened — "I've collapsed, The Voice and I are one" — you can take further steps to free yourself from your captor. Write or speak the exact statements that The Voice is making, but rather than speaking in the first person (which keeps you and The Voice blended), you become The Voice speaking to the wretched, immoral, unredeemable you. Sit up in bed if you are in bed. Speak out loud in your car. Write it all down at your desk, in the kitchen, in the living room. Don't hold anything back: "You asshole. You good-for-nothing. You amoral, dried-up hag. How DARE you . . . ," and as you talk, notice your breathing. Notice your belly. Notice that you've been feeling dead and suddenly you are beginning to feel your energy return (the energy that The Voice has captured from you). The story itself, the words themselves don't matter as much as the energy locked within them. Don't make judgments about the particulars — Oh my God, I just used the word *hag* — simply feel the direct sensations as they arise in your body. *Wow. This feels like a ball of red-hot lava in my chest. Now it's rising into my throat. Now it's going down into my belly, my arms. Now I feel big. Expanded.* Notice what's happening without acting it out. Without indulging it or repressing it. Just energy. Passion itself. Unrestrained. You allow it. After a while, you notice that when this energy is not directed at an object, when you sense the energy without placing it on anyone or anything, you feel alive. You have yourself back. You are sprung. Nameless. Free.

After both disengaging and reclaiming your own strength, you can now discern and make decisions about your discomfort. You might decide that your body doesn't feel good when you eat sugar. That you need to see a doctor or a nutritionist. You might decide that you need to change jobs. Or spouses. That your body needs to move more. But until you are free from The Voice, any decisions you make based on its oppression are like confessions made while being tortured. When you decide that you need to lose twenty pounds because you are disgusting at this weight or that you need to meditate every day or go to church on Sundays because you will go to hell if you don't, you are making life decisions while you are being whipped with chains. The Voice-induced decisions — those made from shame and force, guilt or deprivation, cannot be trusted. They do not last because they are based on fear of consequences instead of longing for truth.

Instead, ask yourself what you love. Without fear of consequences, without force or shame or guilt. What motivates you to be kind, to take care of your body, your spirit, others, the earth? Trust the longing, trust the love that can be translated into action without the threat of punishment. Trust that you will not destroy what matters most. Give yourself that much.

■ ■ ■ ■

# PART THREE:
# EATING

■ ■ ■ ■

# Chapter Eleven:
## Those Who Have Fun and Those Who Don't

My favorite diet of all time was the Cigarette, Coffee and Diet Shasta Creme Soda diet. A prominent psychologist named Bob told me about it one summer when I was a sophomore in college. Bob, who once weighed over four hundred pounds, was now exaltingly thin because of his new invention, the All-Brown Diet: smoking three packs of cigarettes and drinking twelve cups of coffee a day, period.

"Wow!" I said to Bob at a restaurant where I was stuffing myself with popovers slathered with butter and he was, natch, drinking coffee and making perfectly round muted-gray smoke rings. "Finally! A way to be thin!"

Bob bounced his head vigorously. Doused with enough caffeine to run a nuclear power plant, his physical movements verged on maniacal: his feet stamped as he talked, his hands cut circles in the air. Then he said,

"It really works, Geneen. I've lost more than two hundred pounds. And the best part is that there's never a mess to deal with. No chewing to contend with. No dishes to clean. No plates, no silverware. Anyone anywhere can be thin on this diet!"

And so the very next day I went on the All-Brown Diet, with the addition of Diet Shasta creme soda, which was my own unique brown twist. I stayed on the program for three weeks and lost, as you can imagine, a great deal of weight. And since I never slept, I also accomplished many heretofore daunting tasks like reading *The Count of Monte Cristo* and knitting an afghan.

But it wasn't only this program that I greeted with enthusiasm. Every time a new eating regime was brought to my attention — the Fried Chicken Only diet, the One-Hot-Fudge-Sundae-a-Day diet, the All-Grape-Nuts diet — I stepped up to the challenge with enthusiasm, even reverence. I loved being told what to do. It made me feel that someone was in charge. Someone had assessed the situation, understood the mess I was in, and discovered the answer. Protein. Pasta. Raw food. Nightingale droppings. It didn't matter. I was willing to forsake this week's diet for its polar opposite next week because someone said so. I found great comfort in believing that if I could only be faithful and stick to the word, salvation — peace from the relentless self-hatred that I believed was caused by fat thighs — would be mine.

The truth is that every diet I ever went on worked incredibly well. I always lost weight. I always found redemption because the rules were so clear:

- Repent
- Deprive
- Starve

And then I couldn't tolerate the deprivation one more minute. Not one. At the breaking point, I'd become the reverse of myself. Order would flip to chaos, restriction to abandon. Like a werewolf at the full moon, I'd become a creature of the night, a wild thing with little resemblance to the daylight human. I'd rip and tear and crash my way through boxes and cans and bags of food with a voraciousness so intense it was as if I hadn't eaten in years. After eighteen months of living on raw foods and juices, I spent two months inhaling whole pizzas and chunks of salamis. After three weeks on the All-Brown Diet, I spent six weeks chomping on a dozen donuts at a clip. Then, just as suddenly as it started, dawn would break the trance and I'd flip back into being civilized again.

When I stopped dieting I mistakenly assumed that all compulsive eaters craved rules, guidelines, order until they rebelled against them and binged. But about ten years ago, my dietician friend Francie White told me that some people *hate* diets. Some people rebel the second — not three weeks after — they are given a food plan. Their lives are like one long binge.

As I explored this with my students, I discovered that roughly half of them had never been successful on a diet. They weren't interested in rules or order or being told what to do. They told me about the nether world of glazy-dazy eating uninterrupted by restriction. The world of finding themselves at the refrigerator without understanding how they got there. Of finishing a cake before they remembered eating the first bite. It became clear that not all bingeing is driven by deprivation; in half of emotional eaters, bingeing (or, at the very least, consistent overeating) is a way of life punctuated by sleep, work, time with family. Which led me to the conclusion that there are two kinds of compulsive eaters: Restrictors and Permitters.

■ ■ ■ ■

Restrictors believe in control. Of themselves, their food intake, their environments. And whenever possible, they'd also like to control the entire world. Restrictors operate on the conviction that chaos is imminent and steps need to be taken *now* to minimize its impact.

For a Restrictor, deprivation is comforting because it provides a sense of control. If I limit my food intake, I limit my body size. If I limit my body size, I (believe I can) limit my suffering. If I limit my suffering, I can control my life. I make sure that bad things don't happen. That chaos stays away.

The extreme pole of restriction blooms into anorexia — life-threatening starvation — but all Restrictors believe in deprivation, restriction and containment as guiding principles. When we eat together at my retreats, I know the Restrictors immediately: there is more space on their plates than food.

One of their core beliefs is that less is more. If less of me shows, that's less to get hurt. If I cut myself off at the knees, then I won't have far to fall when someone else brings out their sword. Eating less — and therefore being thin — is equated with being safe.

When calories were the measurement of the day, Restrictors knew how many calories were in a small apple, a dish of ice cream, an Oreo cookie. When the au courant measurement switched to the glycemic index, they knew how many grams of fat, protein and carbohydrates were in a piece of toast, a teaspoon of olive oil, a blueberry muffin. What's that, you say? Oat bran is the newest miracle food? Great, I'll put it in everything I eat for the next ten years. Oh? Oat bran causes cancer? Okay, I'll stop eating it immediately. Since restriction/deprivation is translated as control, and since control means safety and safety means survival, any prospect of deprivation elicits relief: Tell me what I need to cut out and I will do it immediately. Tell me what, when, and how much to eat. Give me lists to memorize. Give me the rules and I will be yours forever. My life depends on it.

Since Restrictors are constantly trying to contain the wild energy stomping to be released — the full moon, after all, is always only days way — they can never truly relax. Since they are trying to stave off the inevitable, they have to work very hard, and since they have to work so hard, they have convinced themselves that suffering is noble.

And if it's not hard, it's not worth doing.

They are not exactly a laugh a minute, but laughter and fun are not their goals. For fun (or what passes for it), we turn to their sisters, the Permitters.

Permitters find any kind of rules abhorrent. If they've ever lost weight on a diet, it was through wrenching, abject misery. They are suspicious of programs, guidelines, eating charts.

Permitters say, "I've gained fifty pounds in the last six months and I just can't understand what happened." Whereas a Restrictor operates with hypervigilance, with their antennae in constant motion like those of a sea anemone, Permitters prefer going through life in a daze. That way, they don't need to feel pain — theirs or anyone else's. If I'm not aware of it, there's nothing to fix. If I go through life asleep, I don't need to be concerned about the future because I won't be aware of it. If I give up trying, I won't be disappointed when I fail.

Like Restrictors, Permitters operate on the need to be safe in what they consider hostile or dangerous situations. But unlike Restrictors, who try to manage the chaos, Permitters merge with it. They see no point in trying to control the uncontrollable and have decided that it's best to be blurry and numb and join the party. Have a good time.

In my book *When You Eat at the Refrigerator, Pull Up a Chair,* I wrote about my Permitter friend Sally, whom I called my what-the-hell friend: "No matter how I feel when I arrive at her house I soon find myself thinking, 'Oh, what the hell. Might as well drink champagne from crystal goblets. Might as well paint my toenails gold. Might as well take a bath in the middle of the day in her giant tub with the mermaid spouts. What was I so caught up in before I got here, anyway?' " Being with Sally feels like being on a binge without the food.

Although both Permitters and Restrictors believe that there is not enough to go around, that they won't get what they need, Restrictors react to the perceived lack by depriving themselves before they can be deprived; Permitters react by trying to store up before the bounty/love/attention runs out. They are the ones from whom the (distorted) stereotype of "fat and jolly" derive because they often appear as if they *are* having fun. They look like they are carefree, but only because they refuse to include anything that impinges on their protective orb of numbness. Their lives depend on denial in the same way that Restrictors' lives depend on deprivation — and

184

when your very survival depends on sailing through life by eliminating the lower rungs of truth, it is no longer fun. Or jolly.

Nonetheless, since most of the culture does not delve beneath the world of appearances, it seems as if Permitters have more fun. For a Restrictor, being with a Permitter is like being let out of school for a snow day. It's like being with someone from another planet. When I go to Starbucks with a Permitter friend, I order a small chai tea with organic milk and no water. She orders the biggest possible Frappuccino — not the lite kind — with extra whipped cream. "But it's eleven in the morning," I say. She grins and says, "Life is short, honey, want some whipped cream?"

You might be wondering why Restrictors don't turn in their badges and go to Permitter camp. If you have to be one or the other (and everyone does), why not be a Permitter? Why would anyone deprive themselves when they could drink champagne and eat whipped cream with abandon before noon?

As a Restrictor, I've wondered the same things. But so does every Permitter. When I first introduce this material in my retreats, my students have two main reactions: great relief and bitter envy. Relief at having their behavior named. Envy at wanting to be whatever they're not. Restrictors suddenly believe that their lives would be better if they could relinquish control. But Permitters are convinced that if they could adhere to a reasonable food plan, they could lose weight.

Our subtype is not up to us. As my mother says, it depends on into which bed you were born. We are born with certain innate proclivities, certain twists in our perceptions. Siblings, even twins, with the same parents, the same environments, perceive events differently. In my experience, we are Permitters or Restrictors when we are born; it is that lens through which we see our families.

But fun or no fun, *both* restricting and permitting are outdated, irrelevant relics of behavior that have little value in our lives now. They are, as I've said, survival mechanisms. They are childhood defenses that we are now using to protect ourselves from losses that already happened.

Restricting and permitting are subtypes of compulsive eating, which is the metadefense. A compulsion is a way to protect ourselves from feeling what we believe is unfeelable, what we are convinced is intolerable. It is a compulsion because we are compelled to engage in it. Because in the moment we are acting it out, we believe we have no choice. And while infants and small children are choiceless about the environments in which they've landed and about their options when their caretakers are acting in unkind or abusive ways, adults have a panoply of choices. An infant can turn her head toward or away, that's it. While infants and children cannot tolerate too much suffering without fragmenting, adults with reasonably intact egos and nervous systems do not need to fear that pain will kill them. When we consistently use defenses that we developed twenty or fifty years ago, we freeze ourselves in the past. We lose touch with reality. We live a lie.

Restrictors control. Permitters numb. Both have had brilliant lifesaving strategies of titrating our pain when we were totally dependent on other people and/or helpless to act on our own behalf. But since being vulnerable and open no longer means being shamed, rejected, abused or hurt, permitting and restricting are no longer efficient or adaptive strategies. By constantly laminating our past defenses onto our current reality, we create the illusion that what was there then is here now. We never arrive in the refulgent ever-new possibilities of the present.

Jill Bolte Taylor, a Harvard-trained neuroanatomist, talks about the euphoria she experienced when, during a stroke, her left-brain functions of linear thinking and using the past to orient the present stopped functioning. When there was no longer a memory of the way things were, there was no concept of the self, no longer a me and a you. There was no separation between the molecules in a hand and the molecules in a sink or in a blade of grass. Without the grid of the past imposed on the moment-to-moment unfolding of the present, there was only peace, only radiance, only awareness and profound awe at living itself.

Spiritual teachers have been pointing to that same possibility minus the stroke for thousands of years: the bliss that occurs by arriving where you are. When we are not reconstructing the past in every nanosecond, what is here is so satisfying, so loving, so unbelievably simple that once tasted, it changes everything. Because then you know what's possible and you refuse to settle for anything less.

At a weekend gathering of twenty students in my retreat group, I ask everyone to bring their favorite food to share, saying that I will provide the main course and dessert.

I bring a whole poached salmon and a Chocolate Decadence cake. (As far as I'm concerned, that could be the meal, although I am open to adding some vegetables and lettuce leaves should they appear.)

A feeling of excitement and anticipation sparks the room. Food! Eating! Yes! When everyone has finished placing their food on the table, we have eight loaves of bread, two wheels of cheese, five packages of crackers, two boxes of cookies, one salad, one bag of baby carrots, one carton of cherry tomatoes — and the salmon and chocolate cake.

The Restrictors only want to eat what they brought: the cherry tomatoes, the salads, and the carrots. And they are furious with me for bringing the chocolate cake.

One of them says, "We are supposed to be working here, looking at our *issues,* not having fun."

Another says, "How am I supposed to enjoy my food with that *thing* staring at me?"

But the Permitters are thrilled.

"Where did you get this cake? Do you think they deliver to Wyoming?"

And "How much of this can we take at one time?"

Still another Permitter, she of the recent LAP-BAND operation, says, "I can only take little pieces of it at one time, but is it

189

okay with you if I take many slivers over the next few hours?"

There is nothing like having chocolate cake three inches away to reveal your fear of chaos or your desire to melt into it.

Which is the reason that compulsive eating — and therefore permitting and restricting — is a doorway to what Jill Bolte Taylor calls the euphoria of the present moment. The moment you distinguish between acting out the impulse to move away from the present moment by starving or stuffing and the awareness of the impulse to move away, you are no longer captive to your past.

Awareness and compulsion cannot coexist, since the latter depends on obliteration of the former. With the awareness of the desire to stuff yourself without stuffing yourself, you've stepped out of your immersion in your past and begun arriving in the present: the you that is aware of your past without being it. Once you are here now, you can begin asking yourself what that feels like, sounds like, looks like. You can notice what you've never noticed. It's like suddenly realizing that your favorite music has been playing for hours but you've been so involved in watching videos on YouTube that you haven't heard a note. Or like taking a walk in the forest with earbuds and your iPod and one day realizing that you've missed the crunch of leaves, the birdsong, the smell of the redwood tree.

The beginning always involves noticing where you are and what you are doing. Not trying to be anywhere else. Not, as I tell my students, trying to change one hair on your head. You're sitting in front of a chocolate cake and you notice you want the entire thing now. You don't care whether the band around your small intestine from the operation you just had breaks. You don't care if anyone else in the group gets a piece. You want it all.

Good thing to notice. You don't judge yourself. You don't think that wanting it all means anything about the kind of person you are. You don't tell yourself how selfish you are, and if the others knew that you wanted it all, they'd throw you out. None of that. You bring yourself back to the present moment, and since your body is right here, right now, since hunger or lack of it is also right here, you ask yourself if you are hungry. Simple. *Am I hungry?*

Since Permitters use food to leave their bodies, they are not conversant in the language of hunger and fullness. They eat because it's there and because they feel like it, not because their bodies speak to them.

The antidote to leaving the body is, as always, first to be aware that you've left, and then slowly and gently to return to it. Begin by noticing one breath and then another. Become aware of any tension in your body. Wiggle your feet. Feel the surface of the chair you are sitting on or the earth you are standing on. Little by little, Permitters need to begin recognizing hunger and fullness cues. They need to begin the process of inhabiting their legs, their arms, their bellies.

Restrictors know when they are hungry (except when the pattern goes into the extremes of anorexia and bingeing) and when they have had enough. But eating what they want usually doesn't occur to them. Wanting is scary; it means losing control. And so they begin slowly, with acknowledging foods they might want that are not on the preferred side of their charts. Whole yogurt, for instance, usually makes a Restrictor gasp with horror. Whipped cream can evoke pandemonium. But, as I remind the Restrictors with whom I work, this is just food we're talking about. If the idea of a few puffs of whipped cream has the power to topple your carefully constructed sense of self, we need to discover who you are taking yourself to be. Is it a young child who believes that she needs to manage her environment so that everyone will be happy and she will be safe? Is it the one who believes that the less she has, the less she will get in trouble? When you understand that you are taking yourself to be a child who no longer exists, it is like removing the earbuds and being suddenly aware of the buzz of the ruby-throated hummingbird's wing. You begin the process of noticing what does exist. What is here, now.

A few last words about labels.

Everyone is both Permitter and Restrictor. A Restrictor turns into a Permitter the moment she binges. A Permitter becomes a Restrictor every time she decides that she is going to follow a program, even if that resolution lasts two hours.

Assigning names to complex and multidimensional human behavior is convenient, but it can also be used to distance ourselves from a thorough understanding of the pattern we are naming. We gravitate toward labels because it's always a relief to be seen, to find ourselves in descriptions. But we often end up explaining our behavior with "Oh yeah, I ate like that because I am a Virgo with Scorpio rising who is the adult child of an alcoholic who is also a six on the

Enneagram who is also a Permitter." Labels can become excuses for laziness. "I don't need to be curious about what I do because I already know the reasons for my behavior: I am a Restrictor. If I am rigid about what I eat, it is because Restrictors like structure. Problem solved." What originated as a way to find similarities in a complex list of behaviors becomes a way to dismiss that same behavior as if it is already known and understood.

I introduce the Restrictor-Permitter axis of compulsive eating lightly in my retreats because it is helpful in revealing patterns that have been mystifying or painful. But when my students scramble around trying to fit their behavior into one of those labels or use the labels to justify their eating, I tell them to forget they ever heard the words *Permitter* or *Restrictor*.

If these subtypes reveal something about your relationship with food that was previously eluding you, use them. If the labels confuse you, if you find yourself arguing with them (or me) because you can't find yourself in them, remember that they are only fingers pointing at the sky, not the sky itself.

# CHAPTER TWELVE:
## IF LOVE COULD
### SPEAK

When I first realized how simple it was to end the compulsion with food — eat what your body wants when you're hungry, stop when you've had enough — I felt as if I had popped out of life as I knew it and suddenly found myself in another galaxy. As if I'd been trying to slog through quicksand with lead boots and was now soaring in a world where gravity didn't exist, and all I did — all there ever was to do — was take off the damn boots.

I was convinced that once the word was out, once people realized that they already had the answer to their food woes, the multibillion-dollar diet industry would collapse. We'd reach our natural weights and, no longer consumed by consuming, we'd move on to dismantling nuclear weapons, ending our dependence on oil, and discovering nonsurgical procedures for eyelid droop. Instead, people looked at me with suspicion

— Hunger? What does hunger have to do with eating? — and varying degrees of hostility. Regis Philbin (in the days before my favorite character, Hayley a.k.a. Kelly Ripa from *All My Children,* became his cohost) rolled his eyes and said, "Oh come on, are you saying that if I wanted hot fudge sundaes every day for three weeks I could eat them and lose weight?"

"Um," I said, "well, yes, kind of." Regis was taken aback, momentarily speechless. Besides waiting for an answer, he was probably wondering if I could utter a word that had two syllables. But here, and just a few decades late, is my answer: If you actually listen to what your body (not your mind) wants, you'll discover that it doesn't want three weeks of hot fudge sundaes despite the panting and salivating that is evoked at their very mention. In addition to your body's need for foods other than cream and fudge, there is also the fact that the moment you tell yourself you can have it, the moment the taboo is removed, hot fudge sundaes become as ordinary as sardines. Ask any woman who has fallen for a married or otherwise unavailable lover about this fall from grace. Ask about the passion (and lack of it) when said lover becomes available and she can suddenly have what she thought she wanted. It's an axiom in both love and food that getting what you want is worlds apart from wanting what you can't get.

Most of us have become so entranced with the intransigence of the food-and-weight problem that we cannot see that it is largely due to our refusal to take off the damn boots. We are like the people in the inattentional blindness experiments who are so focused on watching the ball in the basketball game that they never notice the woman in the gorilla costume prancing across the floor.

Those of us who are utterly focused on food and weight never consider that we are ignoring the most obvious solution. We tell ourselves that the answer is out there and our job is to keep looking, to never give up until we find the right solution. One month it's about white foods. Then it's about brain chemistry. Finding the right drug. The fat gene. Being addicted to sugar. Eating for our blood type. Alkaline- and acid-forming foods. Although attending to one or some of these issues might indeed ease our struggle, we use the hunt for answers to abdicate personal responsibility — and with it, any semblance of power — for our relationship with food. Underlying each frenzied bout of passionate involvement in

the newest solution is the same lack of interest in looking down at our own feet. The
same conviction that "I don't have the
power to do anything about this problem."
We want to be done, we want to be fixed.
But since the answer is not where we are
looking, our efforts are doomed to fail.

Freedom from obsession is not about
something you do; it's about knowing who
you are. It's about recognizing what sustains
you and what exhausts you. What you love
and what you think you love because you
believe you can't have it.

During the first few months of soaring
hither and thither without my lead boots,
any food or way of eating (in the car, standing up, sneaking) that spaced me out,
drained my energy, made me feel terrible
about myself soon lost its appeal. On the
other side of the moon, in the galaxy without
gravity, it became apparent that eating was
always about only one thing: nourishing the
body. And this body wanted to live. This
body loved being alive. Loved moving with
some measure of ease. Loved being able to
see, hear, touch, smell, taste — and food
was a big part of how I could do that. The
way I ate was another way to soar.

■ ■ ■ ■

The Eating Guidelines describe what eating looks like when it is another way to soar. When it is relaxed and nourishing, free and life sustaining. I've written extensively about the Guidelines in my first three books, and versions of them have been adapted in other books and co-opted by the diet industry, but they nonetheless still serve as fundamental pointers to intuitive eating. And fascinating doors to how we eat and therefore how we live.

I didn't always find the Guidelines so compelling. When I first taught them, I regarded them as a boring but necessary set of instructions about breaking free from compulsive eating. I'd bought into the prevailing cultural perspective on the obsession with food as a banal woman's problem that needed to be removed like a tick so we could focus on more pressing spiritual, intellectual, and political concerns. But after working with so much suffering in so many women, I believe that the fact that more than half the women in this country are slogging in the quicksand of food obsession *is* a spiritual, intellectual and political concern — which means the Guidelines are a spiritual practice. If those women could unpack their pain (beginning with allowing themselves to use food as a way of supporting rather than punishing themselves) and tell the truth about their lives — to paraphrase poet Muriel Rukeyser — the world would split open.

And a little world-splitting might go a long way since our objectification of matter — including women's bodies — is a partial cause of the apocalyptic disaster in which we now find ourselves. Rather than treating our bodies (and the body of the earth) with reverence, we trash them, try to bend them to our wills. Given the precipice we are now hanging from — whether we refer to the melting glaciers or the childhood obesity rate — we can safely assume that the way we are doing it is not working.

The Guidelines offer another way.

Each one has its nonfood equivalent, its nonapparent or "spiritual" dimension. You can sneak food, for instance, hide what you eat from friends and family, but you can also sneak your true feelings. You can lie to people about what you believe, what you want, what you need. And you can examine your life by either looking at the way you live or the way you eat. Both are paths to what is underneath and beyond the eating:

to what has never gotten hungry, never binged, never gained or lost a pound.

Although Permitters and Restrictors have dramatically different relationships to concrete guidance (from another person) and structure (such as the Eating Guidelines), both the slavish adherence to structure and the utter abhorrence of guidance are reactions that need to be examined. Both Permitters and Restrictors need some sort of compass — even one that is as lightly held as the Eating Guidelines — to wade through the murkiness of compulsion. While it sounds lovely to say, "Just leave yourself alone. Your true nature will take care of everything," too often leaving yourself alone means leaving yourself to your habitual and well-grooved ways of eating. Which means the habitual ways you starve and stuff yourself.

I often get letters from Restrictors-turned-Permitters who are stuck in rebelling against the years of being told what, when and how much to eat. They are as done with anything resembling rules or food plans as they were attached to them before.

Rebelling against some kind of concrete guidance is just the other side of the slavish adherence to it. Either way, you are not free because the rule itself is still determining your behavior.

When Permitters rebel against structure, or when Restrictors turn Permitters and rebel against structure, it's not the structure that is causing so much havoc but the way it is being interpreted. The stories they are telling themselves about it. How they are defining failure, success. Who they take themselves to be. The meaning they give to losing or gaining weight. *My life is lost unless I eat every single time for the next twelve years when I am hungry; I am such a failure that I can't even figure out when I am hungry.*

My retreat students have taught me that no matter how I present them, giving people instructions around food — even when they involve trust and a great deal of chocolate — is always a bit dicey. The Guidelines, despite being pointers to relaxation and freedom, are often viewed as one more set of rules to follow. One more set of rules to throw out. Seven more ways to rebel.

During one lunch break a few years ago, after spending three hours talking about the Guidelines, I moseyed into the dining room where people were descending on their lunches in what can only be described as a feeding frenzy. I watched my beloved students pile their plates with so much food that it made the eating scene in *Tom Jones* look like an advertisement for anorexia.

When I realized my carefully constructed communication about the Guidelines was somewhat lacking in the follow-through department, I rang a bell and asked everyone to put down their silverware. (Warning: Do NOT try this with your friends or families. Unless people are paying you to interrupt their eating, you take the risk of being shot like a moose at Balmoral if you stand between a hungry eater and her food. Even my retreat coteachers — close friends — regard me with savageness when I ring the "put down your silverware" bell.)

Since that fateful afternoon, we spend at least one or two meals a day at the retreats in active exploration of the food on our plates, but that lunchtime was the first. After deflecting a spate of viperous glances and a loud resounding "No!" I got quickly to the point: "We just spent the morning going into great detail about hunger, satisfaction and body signals — namely, the Eating Guidelines. And I am curious about how that is affecting you now."

A dumbfounded silence ensued. Then one person had the courage to say, "What Eating Guidelines?" Another said, "Oh, *those.*

What do those have to do with lunch?"

The next day, in an attempt to defuse the rebellion against a set of perceived rules they believed were masquerading under the name of Guidelines, I started calling them the If Love Could Speak Instructions. I said to my students, "If love could speak to you about food, it would say, 'Eat when you are hungry, sweetheart, because if you don't, you won't enjoy the taste of food. And why should you do anything you don't enjoy?' If love could speak to you, it would say, 'Eat what your body wants, darling, otherwise you won't feel so well, and why should you walk around feeling tired or depressed from what you put into your mouth?' If love could speak to you, my little cream puff, it would say, 'Stop eating when you've had enough, otherwise you will be uncomfortable, and why spend one minute in discomfort?' "

They liked it.

They laughed. They understood that this was in fact what the Guidelines were attempting to do: teach the art of revering themselves with food.

They still rebelled.

They taught me that compulsive eating usually dies a bite-by-bite death. You hear about the Guidelines (or the If Love Could

Speak Instructions, whichever you prefer) and you think, Wow! I could do that! Then you discover that you get a kick out of sneaking food, and you can't stop grazing at the refrigerator, and maybe being compulsive isn't so bad after all. But once you glimpse the possibility of freedom, taste the ease of soaring, you can't go back. Once you know, you can't unknow.

Still.

Love speaks, but you might not feel like listening. At any moment on a particular afternoon, you might be more interested in using food as a drug, in eating the entire cake. That's the way it's going to go for a while. My recommendation is to start slowly. (If you make these instructions into yet another project to undertake — like going to the gym five days a week after lumping around for six years — you will puff yourself up and quickly feel deflated.) Notice which instructions you feel aligned with and which you'd rather forget about. Pick one that appeals to you. Be aware of it during the week. Notice what it's like to follow it and what it's like to ignore it.

Trust the process, trust your longing for freedom. Eventually you will stop wanting to do anything that interferes with the increasing brightness you have come to associate with being alive And rest assured that like the butterfly that flutters its wings in one part of the world and causes a hurricane in another, every time a woman aligns her eating with relaxation, every time she takes off her damn boots, the laces fly open for the rest of us.

# CHAPTER THIRTEEN: BEING HOT FUDGE SUNDAES

The Eating Guidelines are like nested Russian dolls; they are exactly what they appear to be and they are also worlds opening endlessly onto other worlds. It's possible, for instance, to interpret the Eat What Your Body Wants Guideline only as it relates to food. A noticeable progression will unfold: you might start off by eating everything in sight and then realize that everything in sight is a reaction, a rebellion to the unspoken rule that you are not allowed to have what you want. But when you tell yourself you can have what you want, the rule collapses — and with it, any reaction to it. You find yourself slowly discovering foods you and your body actually want. What foods energize you, awaken you, sustain you. Once you realize that it's possible to feel good by not eating certain things and including others instead, the compulsion begins to fall away because you've found something bet-

207

ter: getting your life back. The progression from eating wildly to eating to nourish your life force varies from person to person, but if you find yourself eating everything that doesn't eat you first for longer than a few weeks, you're using this Guideline as an excuse to binge.

Eat What Your Body Wants also includes wanting that is longing — an expression of the heart's desire — which includes beauty and yearning to know what is beyond the world of appearances. "All wanting — for love, to be seen for who we are, for a new red car," John Tarrant writes, "is wanting to find and be taken into this mysterious depth in things." In a letter to Albert Einstein, a child wrote, "I want to know what is beyond the sky. My mother said you could tell me." By collapsing the whole of our wanting into something as tangible as butterscotch pudding, we cancel poetry, sacredness, longing from our lives and resign ourselves to living with hearts banged shut. The simple instruction to Eat What Your Body Wants begins to pry open what has been hidden for a lifetime.

From a retreat student:

Every time I eat, it's like I'm confirming the secret knowledge that I am just a bad girl deep down, that love and beauty are not meant for me, that I'm alone and doomed and destined to stay in this perpetual purgatorial zone. Going along, doing good work in the world, engaging with my community, but always returning to the cold, hard truths of this dry loneliness and the inherent limitations of my life. Despite the reality that there is so much available to me, I keep overeating to forbid myself from having it, and also to comfort myself because I feel like I don't deserve it or am not allowed to have it.

I perpetuate my beliefs by eating. One of the things I noticed on Sunday during our eating meditation was how, when I was eating, I felt my chest — my heart — physically clenching. I felt bad about eating, and I felt like someone might take it away, or that I would take it away from myself, so I clenched myself. It's as if I've constructed a heart wall that no one can cross, that no intimacy can penetrate. I keep people out and one of the main ways I do that is by eating.

I am beginning to understand that this whole struggle with food is not about discipline or self-control or bargaining with myself; it's not even about food. It is a

story — a powerful story — about loving
and wanting and having.

In the first few weeks of eating what I
wanted, I confused what I hadn't allowed
myself to eat without guilt with what my
body wanted. And since I had been dieting
for seventeen years, my list of forbidden
foods was long. (Although I had been bingeing for as long as I'd been dieting, binges
were never free. After the second and third
bites, they became exercises in self-torture
and guilt, like cutting myself with a knife,
hurling myself into walls. Every binge left
me scarred and desperate and sick.)

When I told myself that this time I could
eat what I wanted with no strings attached
— no threat of a diet on any Monday morning for the rest of my life — I headed
straight for the foods of my childhood I was
never allowed to eat. It was as if in letting
myself eat what I couldn't eat as a kid, I
thought I could get what I never got. As if
in redoing the food part of the story, I could
redo the plot in which it developed; by eating ice cream instead of ice milk, cookies
instead of graham crackers, I was secretly
planning to have a second childhood, with
June and Ward Cleaver for parents.

And as I've written before, I was so elated

with my resolve to never diet again that I didn't notice that I was bumping around in a sugar haze from eating only raw and cooked chocolate-chip cookies. I needed to prove to myself that what I wanted most was not forbidden, but what I didn't understand was that I didn't want the cookies; I wanted the way being allowed to have them made me feel: welcomed, deserving, adored.

It's never been true, not anywhere at any time, that the value of a soul, of a human spirit, is dependent on a number on a scale. We are unrepeatable beings of light and space and water who need these physical vehicles to get around. When we start defining ourselves by that which can be measured or weighed, something deep within us rebels.

We don't want to *eat* hot fudge sundaes as much as we want our lives to *be* hot fudge sundaes. We want to come home to ourselves. We want to know wonder and delight and passion, and if instead we've given up on ourselves, if we've vacated our longings, if we've left possibility behind, we will feel an emptiness we can't name. We will feel as if something is missing because something is missing — the connection to the source of all sweetness, all love, all power, all peace, all joy, all stillness. Since we had it once — we were born with it — it can't help but haunt us. It's as if our cells remember that home is a jeweled palace but we've been living as beggars for so long that we are no longer certain if the palace was a dream. And if it was a dream, then at least we can eat the memory of it.

During the first few bites, and before we get dazed by overeating, everything we want is possible. Everything we've lost is here now. And so we settle for the concrete version of our lost selves in the form of food. And once food has become synonymous with goodness or love or fulfillment, we cannot help but choose it, no matter how high the stakes are. No matter if our doctor tells us that we won't live another month at this weight. Because when we are lost, when we are homeless, when we've spent years separated from who we are, threats of failed hearts or joint pressure don't move us. Dying does not frighten those who are already half dead.

The prince in Mark Twain's classic novel *The Prince and the Pauper,* while dressed in rags, kept proclaiming: I am the King, I am the King, you can't control me! He remained steadfast about his royal heritage even when no one believed him, even when he was thrown in jail. But most of us have spent so many years questioning our right to take up space that we only know one way to be heard: I am the Queen, I am the Queen, you can't control what I eat! After years of confusing spiritual and physical hunger, and after years of telling ourselves that who we are is what we weigh, we are excruciatingly sensitive to being told what and when and how much to eat. It's as if, at some level, our unfettered but as yet unconscious radiance perks its head up and says "I will not be caged. I will not be restrained."

The most challenging part of any system that addresses weight-related issues is that unless it also addresses the part of you that wants something you can't name — the heart of your heart, not the size of your thighs — it won't work. We don't want to be thin because thinness is inherently life-affirming or lovable or healthy. If this were true, there would be no tribes in Africa in which women are fat and regal and long-lived. There would be no history of matriarchies in which women's fecundity and sheer physical abundance were worshipped. We want to be thin because thinness is the purported currency of happiness and peace and contentment in our time. And although that currency is a lie — the tabloids are filled with miserable skinny celebrities — most systems of weight loss fail because they don't live up to their promise: weight loss does not make people happy. Or peaceful. Or content. Being thin does not address the emptiness that has no shape or weight or name. Even a wildly successful diet is a colossal failure because inside the new body is the same sinking heart. Spiritual hunger can never be solved on the physical level.

A famous Zen master said, "There is no right. There is no wrong. But right is right and wrong is wrong."

The same is true of the Eating Guidelines. Following them does not lead you to a life free from emotional eating. But you cannot free yourself from the obsession with food without following them. Food has a direct effect on our appetite and willingness to inquire, to discern what is true, to do the work of returning ourselves to what we love. Food — as matter turned to spirit — is the direct connection between the physical and the spiritual, between what we put in our mouths and what we feel in our hearts. Passion, strength, joy cannot take root in exhausted, burdened, half-dead bodies.

■ ■ ■ ■

In my workshops we do a simple eating exercise: people are given a small cup with three different foods in it. One day, it is a grape, a piece of graham cracker, and a piece of Dove dark chocolate. The day before, it is a Hershey's Kiss, a tortilla chip, and two raisins. I've been doing a version of this exercise as long as I've been teaching, and every time — every single time — the effect is startling, because when you eat just one of something slowly, looking at it, holding it up to the light, rubbing it on your lips, rolling it around in your mouth, all the hopes and dreams and fantasies you've overlaid onto food become apparent. One person said, "One is enough but when I think about all the other ones in the bag, I feel as if I am missing so much. As if big love is waiting for me and by eating just one, I am turning it down." We both knew that what she was saying was not literally true. That if she ate the whole bag, she'd be missing not love but any semblance of feeling well. Still, her beliefs about deprivation and having enough were so laminated onto food that unless she was willing to be curious about what food was representing, she'd

215

continue to believe that a bag of Hershey's Kisses held the way to the promised land.

You have to be willing to go all the way. To understand that food is a stand-in for love and possibility and whatever you call true nature or God. Otherwise you will keep gaining and losing weight for the rest of your life. You will keep wringing your hands and lamenting and feeling like a victim. And although, as I say to my students, you wouldn't be alone if you chose to spend your life that way — most people who struggle with food and weight do exactly that — it is at least helpful to understand that the choice is yours to make. You get to decide what you are going to do with, as Mary Oliver writes, "your one wild and precious life."

The Eating Guidelines sound like a list of things to do — and on the most obvious level, they are — but they are also a description of unbounded freedom that is always a bite away. The Guidelines are a path to the view site and they are also the breathtaking view. They are the means to the end of obsessive eating, and they are descriptions of what the end looks and feels like. They are always true because they describe truth as it expresses itself through food.

Living with the Guidelines is itself a spiritual practice because it takes presence, awareness and the immediacy of being in the moment to follow them. I often tell my students that if, at the beginning, all they can manage is to be aware of the Guidelines when they eat — even if only for five minutes — they will be contacting that which is greater than their conflicting desires and conditioned responses to deprivation and old hungers. When even a moment of that "spiritual" part of them is experienced with food, there is a natural inclination to want to keep exploring, keep discovering, keep touching the place that has never known suffering — which is, after all, the function of any spiritual practice.

Seven years ago, a first-time retreat student referred to herself as "a damaged seed." She was a glorious and successful writer, involved in a relationship with a man she loved, but her feelings about herself were dark and conflicted and her weight was their outermost expression.

After a few years of coming to retreats, she "woke up" to herself. She suddenly realized she had choices about what to do with her time, how to live her life. She began saying no. To people she didn't want to be with, to places she didn't want to go. "I even

217

said no to the Whiners and Diners," she said — a group of seven women who had been meeting once a year for twenty years to eat together and complain about their thighs, arms, bellies. "It's as if I suddenly realize that I don't have to prove anything to my mother anymore. And it's a whole different life. A bright life." She said that "before now, feeling well was not a priority. Not important. Not even a consideration. Why would anyone who believes she's a damaged seed also believe that she deserves to feel fabulously well? But now, I've slowed down. I'm following the Eating Guidelines but not because they're the Guidelines; I'm following them because they are the only ways of eating that make sense."

Spiritual teachers from every tradition describe a profound stillness that is the unvarnished truth of anyone's — everyone's — true nature. But it needs to be broken down in bits by using words and practices because it's too big to assimilate, especially when people are totally convinced of the damage at their core. The purpose of a spiritual path or religion is to provide a precise and believable way into what seems unbelievable.

In the food and weight arena, the Eating Guidelines are both the spiritual and physical practice. They provide a precise path to the world of being in the moment as well as a concrete path to feeling well. They are descriptions of what eating would look like if you had no problem with it at all. You'd listen to your body. You'd eat to nourish yourself. You'd love yourself with food. The Guidelines are exactly what you will come around to when you get tired of aching joints. Of lugging yourself around. The Guidelines are nothing more than understanding that your body is yours and you can eat as a way to be yourself. After all these years, all these diets, all these pounds gained and lost and lost and gained, after eating to resist and rebel and fight, you realize that eating can finally be — and always was — for you, only you.

# Chapter Fourteen:
# The "Oh Shit"
## Mantra

When Mahatma Gandhi was shot, the words that spilled out of his mouth were "Ram, Ram" (a Hindu name for an incarnation of God). He'd been saying that mantra for so long that even when a bullet entered his body, it spilled out of his mouth. I've heard it said that the great American mantra, the first thing that anyone says when faced with a difficult situation — a car crash, a crisis, death — is "Oh shit." And the reason I believe that is because when my students first see the Guidelines they almost always say, "Oh shit."

"Oh shit. I don't want to."

"Oh shit. I have to give up reading *People* magazine at the dinner table."

"Oh shit. No way. You can't make me."

The situation with food is ensconced in our minds in polar opposites. Either I can have what I want or I can't. Either food is fun and I eat compulsively or it's not and I lose weight. One way I suffer, the other way I don't. We hear a Guideline and we immediately think, Deprivation. Trouble. No.

I don't see it that way. When a diabetic tells me that she can't eat what she wants because what she wants will kill her (and therefore she feels deprived), my response is that what will kill her is wanting another life than the one she has, another condition than the one that is hers. Hell is the lack of connection between the thought that she wants to eat the entire cake and the reality that eating the cake would send her into a diabetic coma. It's not the Guideline that needs to be examined, it's her argument with reality. It's not her eating that is killing her, it's her refusal to accept her situation.

A retreat student says, "The Guideline about eating without distractions doesn't work for me. I can't digest my food without reading *The New Yorker* and I don't want to stop."

"So, tell me why you came to the retreat," I say.

"Because I keep overeating. Because I am miserable. Because I can't seem to get a grip on my life."

"What happens at the table when you read?"

"Well, I get so involved in what I read that

I don't notice how much I am eating."

"If reading and eating leads you to overeat, and if overeating is making you miserable, tell me again why you need to read and eat."

"Because I want to," she says defiantly. "Because it makes me happy. Because I live alone and feel lonely if I don't."

"So you're reading to avoid feeling lonely?"

"Yes, I suppose you could say that."

"And how are eating alone and loneliness connected?"

"Duh." She rolls her eyes, as if to say, "Who doesn't know that people who live and eat alone are automatically lonely?"

Silence.

Then: "Anyone knows that people who are living alone at fifty-two years old are losers. Complete losers. When I read and eat, I don't have to face the fact that I am a loser."

"So it's not eating alone that is so painful, and it's not even that eating alone directly leads to loneliness. It's what you tell yourself about eating alone that is so painful. It's the story you tell. It's the nightmare you keep repeating that's making you feel terrible. I'd feel terrible, too, if I had that story going around in my head."

"Wait a second," she says. "I'm not about

to be talked out of reading *The New Yorker.* It gives me pleasure."

"That's fine," I say. "You won't stop doing anything until you are ready. And if reading and eating brings you pleasure, then you shouldn't give it up. The purpose of the Guidelines is to add more pleasure to your life, not less. But it would be good to notice the whole story, not just a corner of it: eating and reading doesn't only bring you pleasure. It also causes you pain. It's not either/or."

People often tell me that my approach is too hard. It's too hard to be aware. It's too hard to eat without distractions. It's too hard to stop when they've had enough. And I say awareness might be hard because it's developing a new skill but not being aware is hard, too. The Eating Guidelines may be challenging because they question familiar, comforting grooves, but not following the Guidelines — eating in the car while talking on the cell phone, steering, putting on lip liner, and trying to get a hunk of hamburger in your mouth while not dripping the ketchup all over your jacket — is a bit challenging as well.

The same is true with feelings. My students will often say to me, "But if I follow the Guidelines and don't eat to push down my sadness, then I have to feel it — and then what?" Before I answer the "then what" part, I point out that the sadness is already present and that the only thing that eating does is add yet another source of sadness: after the food is gone, the original source of sadness is still there except that now they have topped it with the sadness or frustration or hopelessness about their conflicted relationship with food. Contrary to their fantasies, eating has not taken away their sadness — it's doubled it.

There are many ways to deprive yourself: You can deprive yourself of cookies or you can deprive yourself of feeling well after you eat them. You can deprive yourself of feeling your sadness or you can deprive yourself of the confidence and well-being that come from knowing you won't be destroyed by feeling it.

The truth is that eating any other way than the one that the Eating Guidelines describe is a kind of eating in which you've been kidnapped, held hostage by old experiences of deprivation and lack and absence. Any argument you have with the Eating Guidelines is an argument with the past. With your history. It's an argument from an old part of yourself that is determined to get what she didn't get, to have what was denied her, to show anyone who will listen — her parents, her brother, her ninth-grade boyfriend — that she did — she really really did — deserve to be noticed or seen or loved or appreciated.

I say to my students, "Tell me how old you are when, as a diabetic, you want sugar. When you need to read and eat so that the scary monsters in your mind don't ruin your life. Who is the one that wants to eat unending sweets? Is it the four-year-old who is having a tantrum? Is it the eight-year-old who has just been told she is chubby? Who is actually running your life?"

It's not about food. It's never about food. And it's not even about feelings. It's about what's below them. What's in between them. What's beyond them. It's about the parts of you that you take to be you. The parts of you with which you identify. Sometimes I ask my students to tell me about the person they are referring to in "I-me-mine." I ask them to tell me her needs, her wants, her beliefs. And every time — 100 percent of the time — the person they describe is a construct, a mental fabrication, a fantasy image. It's based on inference, history, conditioning. It's based on who they took themselves to be because of what their parents told them, how they were treated, who did and didn't love them. Over time, a set of inferences coalesce into what psychologists call a "self-representation," or self-image, and it is that self-image that we take to be ourselves. When we talk about "feeling like ourselves," we are referring to this compilation of memories and other people's reactions to us — many of which took place before we knew our own names.

When I first realized that my entire definition of myself — who I took myself to be — was basically a figment in my parents' imagination, I was both stunned and elated. I'd been convinced of my own worthlessness for so many years that I'd stopped questioning it and grew like a tree twisting over its deformities.

My mother had spent years telling me I was selfish, and it was upon that nub of information that I built a monument to deficiency. But as I widened the myopic gaze on I-me-mine, I saw my mother at age twenty-five with two small children, a loveless marriage and a desperate need to have a different life. With the little information she had, and doing the very best she could do, she called me selfish for wanting more than she could give. And since I would have died for her, and since every child needs her parents to be right, I took myself to be the sum of her limitations. I saw myself through the eyes of a lonely, depressed, troubled woman — and never questioned my loyalty to her vision. And then there was my father who saw me as a ditzy dumb blonde. Add ditzy dumb blonde to "selfish, fat, unlovable" and you have who I took myself to be for almost fifty years.

Psychologists and spiritual teachers alike call this learned version of ourselves "ego" or "personality" or "false self." It's false because it's based on inference, not direct experience. It's false because if your idea of yourself is based on who your mother took you to be, and her idea of herself was based on who her mother took her to be, which was based on who *her* mother took her to be, your idea of yourself — the person whose feelings get hurt, who takes offense at being criticized, who is wedded to her opinions or preferences or ideas — is based on those of someone who's never met you. Your self-image is refracted so many times — with learned inferences and memories and conditioning — that it is nothing more than a hall of mirrors.

Talk about a great hoax. You are not who you think you are. Hardly anyone is. Because although kids come into this world with an implicit understanding of who they

are, they have no self-reflective conscious-
ness. They know who they are but they
don't know that they know. And the only
way they find out is by seeing themselves in
their parents' eyes. We become what and
who our parents saw. Figments of their
imagination. Then, as my teacher Jeanne
says, we spend our lives following instructions given to us ten or thirty or fifty years
ago by people we wouldn't ask for street
directions from today.

So when people tell me that they need to
eat and read otherwise they will die, I ask
them which part of them will die. Is it the
part that believes that fifty-two-year-olds
are losers if they eat alone? When did they
learn that? Who told them that? Because
being fed was one of the first ways we knew
we were loved, and because we were totally
dependent on our parents to survive, questioning the tangle of food and love beliefs
can often feel like life and death. *I will die if I
don't get that chocolate now. I will die if I can't
eat and read.* The truth is that it is only your
beliefs about yourself that will die. Your
ancient outmoded prehistoric version of
yourself will die. But as long as you are taking yourself to be the two- or eight- or ten-
year-old who needs to believe her mother to
survive, reading *People* magazine or eating

in your car will feel as important to you as breathing.

It's no wonder, then, that people say, "Oh shit" when they see the Guidelines.

Working with the obsession with food is, most of all, working with your loyalty to your old, false, egoic self, since any argument you have with the Guidelines is not coming from a current version of yourself. Let's face it: It doesn't take a rocket scientist to understand that if you are eating at the refrigerator, you are not really being as kind to yourself as you could be. If you are eating in your car while also making sure you don't bump into the car in front of you, it's hard to taste the food. And if you are telling yourself that broken cookies don't count because when the cookies break the calories break, you are being cute (okay, very cute), but you are also lying to yourself. When you edge a cake, when you cut tiny little pieces off the sides every time you walk by and you walk by a dozen times during a day, and you tell yourself that these tiny slices don't really add up to one whole piece of cake, you are lying to yourself. You want the cake but you don't want to want the cake, so you're figuring out how to get it without admitting to yourself that you're eating it.

When you say you want to lose weight but you consistently eat past being satisfied, and when you say you don't know what being satisfied feels like, you are not telling yourself the truth. Satisfaction with food is not difficult to feel but it does take attention. It does take being willing to slow down because it can happen in midbite, and if you are busy reading or driving or watching television, you will miss it. So when you ignore what could help you stop eating emotionally, you have to ask yourself if you really want to stop. And if you then worry that not finishing the food on your plate is a slap in the face of all the hungry people everywhere, you are not living in reality. The truth is that you either throw the food out or you throw it in, but either way it turns to waste. World hunger will not be solved by finishing the garlic mashed potatoes on your plate.

The Guidelines are intuitive, simple, direct. A child of four could follow them. A child of four *does* follow them. Before there was any such thing as instructions that point you back to the basic messages of your body, there was a time when it wouldn't have occurred to you to listen to anything but.

At every first meeting people say to me, "But I work in an office in which lunch breaks are set — how can I eat when I am hungry?" Or "I have three small children under the age of six and it's going to be a thousand years before there is anything resembling a calm environment in my house — so how can I eat without distractions?"

Everyone has situations. Everyone has a life in which a reinterpretation of the Guidelines needs to take place. You may need to adjust your eating schedule so that you are hungry when it is your lunch break. Or you may need to take a walk during your lunch break and eat something small and portable during another short break. You may need to speak to a nutritionist or a doctor to explore what your particular body needs and wants. You may need to eat alone once a week or once a day so that you get acquainted with different levels of hunger: when it first comes on, when it is mild and when it is so severe that you are willing to eat anything that doesn't eat you first. Everyone has situations. But figuring those out is not the hard part.

The hard part is allowing yourself to know what you already know. What you knew when you were four years old but have since forgotten. The hard part is disengaging from

231

the roar of can'ts and won'ts and let-me-outta-heres, from the habitual way you swing into gear around the food thing to paying attention to the deeper song, the deeper truth: you without your story of you. You as you experience yourself directly, here, now. When you sit down, when you listen, when you sense your body directly, there is what Eckhart Tolle calls "animating presence" blazing through you. It is beyond any story. It is not of the past, not anything that anyone ever told you. It's been in the background every minute of your life, but since you were paying attention to the foreground, to the changing appearances and dramas and feelings, you never noticed it. But now you can. And your relationship with food can be the doorway.

There is a discernible inner weather pattern — a combination of feelings and events — that defines and reminds us of our place in the world. And struggling with food is part of it. You believe that you are someone who will always want what you can't have, whether it's thinner thighs or a life without obsession, and then you see the Guidelines and something in you says, *Oh shit. No way.* That's understandable. Obsessions are made of nos. Being free from the obsession is the act of questioning the no. Of relating to your relationship with food instead of from it and as it.

The obsession will end when you love discovering your true nature more than you love being loyal to your mother or father. The obsession will end because you care enough about yourself to stop damaging yourself with food. Because you love yourself enough to stop hurting yourself. Who doesn't want to take care of what they love?

If you pay attention to when you are hungry, what your body wants, what you are eating, when you've had enough, you end the obsession because obsessions and awareness cannot coexist. When you pay attention to yourself, you notice the difference between being tired and being hungry. Between being satisfied and being full. Between wanting to scream and wanting to eat.

The more you pay attention, the more you fall in love with that which is not obsessed: that which is blazing itself through you. The life force that animates your body. Food becomes a way to sustain that blaze, and any way of eating that keeps you depressed or spaced out or uncomfortable loses its appeal. When that happens, you slowly realize that you are being lived by that which is God and you wouldn't have it any other way.

# Epilogue:
## Last Words

It is the last morning of the retreat. The eighty women who wanted to wrap duct tape around my mouth six days ago are now wishing they could camp out in the meditation hall until the next retreat. A Chicago woman says, "I wanted to kill you in those eating meditations; every time you told me to put my fork down and notice if I was hungry, I thought, 'I'm bigger than her; one little snap of her neck and I'd be able to eat my damn pancakes in peace.' Now I'd like to live with you forever. Would Matt mind?"

I don't take it personally. I know the change in the group is not because of anything I've done, but because of what they've seen, felt, experienced: there's nothing like realizing you don't like the food you've been bingeing on for thirty years. Or tasting a strawberry for the first time in your life. Or understanding that your pain won't kill you. That you are more than your stories, more than your personality, and that no situation is unworkable, ever.

But there is also fear in the room. Once you discover joy, you always want it. Once you discover freedom, you want to capture it, never let it go. And so I take this last morning to speak about the basic message of the work: it's not about food or feelings, but it's also not about any particular state. Hatred is as welcome as happiness. Loneliness is as intriguing as ecstasy. Big openings are sometimes followed by big closings, but as long as you are as curious about your disappointment as you are thrilled about your joy, you will not need to use food as a drug. Obsession is an unexpected path because it relentlessly points you back to yourself; whenever you want to eat when you are not hungry or don't want to stop when you've had enough, you know something is occurring that needs your kindness and attention.

"Some people have to go to India," I tell my students. "Some people believe they need gurus or esoteric practices. But you have food — and it is your greatest teacher. If you are willing to engage with yourself rather than run from yourself, and if you are willing to be steadfast and not get seduced by the newest greatest diet, you already have what people go to India to get. Right there on your plate, right smack in the middle of your day-to-day life, you have your way back to the truth." I'm not really saying anything different than I've said for the past six days, but since they've spent hours in silence, hours in the dining room noticing the reasons they eat beside hunger, they know for themselves that what they came here to get rid of is itself the path to what many people call God.

The hard part is not big starry openings, as dramatic and sought-after as they are. Insights, especially on retreat — when every moment of the day is set up to support the inner world — are daily occurrences. But then the women go home (or you finish the book) and the process of connecting the realizations with day-to-day reality begins: remembering the Eating Guidelines, sensing your body, putting aside time every morning to sit quietly, disengaging from The Voice, learning and practicing inquiry. Real change happens bit by bit. It takes great effort to become effortless at anything. There are no quick fixes.

The writer Natalie Goldberg says that we are always practicing something and most of us practice suffering. Why not practice ending your suffering instead of perpetuating it? Since you are eating anyway, moving around in your body anyway, being aware of something anyway, why not spend that time waking yourself up instead of deadening yourself? Is there anything better to do with a life?

A student who has been coming to the retreats for many years says:

I am living the same life, with the same family, and same job as I had before the retreats, yet I am not the same person doing the same things. I feel again and it isn't destroying me. I thought I was "feeling" before, but mainly I was just experiencing my life in reaction mode — a constant distraction to my true experiences/feelings. Many years of misusing food, overexercising, overworking, using drugs/alcohol. Self-destruction felt like home. But now, this body, this life, feels like home.

Until now, I have only been able to access a certain kind of love by thinking about my children. My four-year-old daughter says: "I love you six hundred cats, to the moon and back, and ten pancake breakfasts." And what I am saying is that I am learning to love myself five billion universes, nine hundred and ten strawberries, and three million elephant kisses. It's a completely different life when I direct that kindness toward myself.

There are predictable stages in using food as a doorway to God that are much like what the Sufis describe as the Three Journeys of the Spiritual Path: the Journey from God, the Journey to God and the Journey in God.

In the Sufi version, the Journey from God is the one in which you believe you are what you do, weigh, achieve, and so you spend your time attempting to adorn yourself with external measures of worth: a thin body, a big bank account, cool patent leather boots. Since even thin, rich and famous people get old, have cellulite and die, the journey from God ends in disappointment 100 percent of the time.

In the food version of this journey — the Journey from Yourself — you spend years, sometimes a whole life, dieting, fasting, bingeing, exercising and then laying on the couch because you refuse to do one more situp or downward-facing dog. During this stage your main goal is to fix yourself, reach your ideal weight and rid yourself forever of the focus on food. Since the relationship with food is only a microcosm for your relationship to the rest of your life (and your beliefs about abundance, deprivation, fear, benevolence, God), any attempts to change the food part without also engaging in the beliefs it represents will, like the Sufi version, also end in disappointment 100 percent of the time.

According to the Sufis, the next journey — the Journey to God — is also fraught with disappointment. You try to stop the endless stream of thoughts and they keep playing their crazy tunes. You decide you are going to stamp out judgment, evil, anger, hatred, and you find yourself wishing your next-door neighbor would accidentally slip on a banana peel and die. You find a spiritual guide who seems to be the embodiment of wisdom and purity and he ends up sleeping with sixteen of his flock.

In the food world, this Journey to Yourself is equally as frustrating. You stop dieting. You begin eating what your body wants. You realize your eating isn't about lack of willpower but lack of understanding. As much as you want to lose weight, you suddenly realize that keeping the weight on — and keeping the problem going — is familiar and comforting. You don't want to let go of either the weight or the drama that surrounds it. You've spent your life agonizing about your weight and now, when the end is in sight, you run the other way.

The third journey — the Journey in God — is the same in both the Sufi tradition and the path-of-food version: In this journey, you end the search for more and better. You no longer live as if this life is a dress rehearsal for the next. Authenticity, not trying to be good, begins to infuse your actions. Through practices like the Eating Guidelines, meditation and inquiry, you slowly realize that you are already whole and that there is no test to pass, no race to finish; even pain becomes another doorway, another chance to recognize where love appears to be absent.

When you look at the world through shattered lenses, the world looks shattered. When you eat a particular way because you believe that you are wrong if you don't, freedom isn't free. When you are still bound by beliefs about good and bad, it doesn't matter what you eat or what you weigh — you are still flailing around in the obsession. You are still paying for taking up space in pounds of flesh. Unless you slow down, unless you are actually interested in the beliefs and the needs you are piling on top of the food, you continue to live in a limbo world in which the taste of food is all you know of heaven and the size of your thighs is all you know of hell.

But it doesn't have to be this way. The real holiness is not in what you achieve or eat or weigh. There is something better than endlessly pushing the boulder of obsession up the mountain: putting it down. And if you are willing to refrain from dieting and needing an instant solution, and if you want to use your relationship with food as the unexpected path, you will discover that God has been here all along. In the sorrow of every ending, in the rapture of every beginning. In the noise and in the stillness, in the upheavals and in the rafts of peace. In each moment of kindness you lavish upon your breaking heart or the size of your thighs, with each breath you take — God has been here. She is you.

# ACKNOWLEDGMENTS

Without my retreat students, this book would never have been written. Thank you to every one of you, especially those who allowed me to use their words and stories verbatim. Menno de Lange, Chohan Jane Neale and Loren Matthews, my fabulous team, make teaching each retreat a world of true support and sheer joy. The unflappable Judy Ross coordinates every detail with grace. And a huge thank-you to Premsiri Lewin, Glenn Francis and Sara Hurley for their unforgettable contributions along the way.

Anne Lamott and Kim Rosen shaped the manuscript with their impeccability and wisdom. Thank you for being my friends and for saving me from (and leading me back to) myself. Also, without Maureen Nemeth, my office manager, I'd probably still be crashing around in that back room with the mice and ten thousand slips of paper.

Big splashy gratitude to Ned Leavitt, my agent, for being one of God's biggest fans; Dan Smetanka for staying with me on a rocky ride; Whitney Frick for huge insight; Susan Moldow for believing in the book; and Beth Wareham for being the outrageous editor of my dreams, pom-poms and all. Rosemary Ellis, Jenny Cook, Denise Foley and Judy Stone at *Good Housekeeping* go a long way to easing this writer's heart on a monthly basis.

For undying love, I thank Jeanne Hay forever. My life is completely different because of the Ridhwan School, and I will always be grateful to Hameed Ali and the team of teachers, including Alia Johnson, Deborah Ussery and Morton Letofksy. My Buddhist teachers throughout the years — Joseph Goldstein, Jack Kornfield, Stephen Levine, Lama Yeshe, Lama Zopa, Gonpo Tseden and Dan Brown — introduced me to, and sustained my love for, awareness itself. Catherine Ingram is still soaring with me in that palace of starlight. Barbara Renshaw helped me in profound, practical and life-altering ways too many to name.

For the many dimensions of love and well-being that they each bring to my life, I thank

Jace Schinderman, Taj Inayat, Mayuri Oner-heim, Sandra Maitri, Roseanne Annoni, Rick Foster, Greg Hicks, Allison Post, Karen Johnson and my mother, Ruth Wiggs.

Out of all the people on all the earth, I have the privilege of spending my life with Matt Weinstein. Being loved by you is like living in unstinting shine, like being married to amazement himself.

# ADDENDUM

ADDENDUM

# BEGINNING INQUIRY

Inquiry can be done any time, anywhere — when you are alone, with a friend, with a teacher. When I first teach inquiry in the retreats, I teach it as a writing practice. I ask people to begin by becoming aware of a question — something they don't know but want to know. If they are aware of a problem they have, but think they know why they have it and what to do about it, there is no reason to do inquiry. The effectiveness of inquiry lies in its open-endedness, its evocation of true curiosity.

When you practice inquiry, you see what and who you have been taking yourself to be that you have never questioned. Inquiry allows you to be in direct contact with that which is bigger than what you are writing about: the infinite unexplored worlds beyond your everyday discursive mind.

Here are the instructions I give to my students:

- Give yourself twenty minutes in which you won't be disturbed.
- Sense your body. Feel the surface you are sitting on. Notice the point of contact your skin is making with your clothes. Be aware of your feet as they touch the floor. Feel yourself inhabiting your arms, your legs, your chest, your hands.
- Ask yourself what you are sensing right now — and where you are sensing it. Be precise. Do you feel tingling? Pulsing? Tightening? Do you feel warmth or coolness? Are the sensations in your chest? Your back? Your throat? Your arms?
- Start with the most compelling sensations and ask these questions: Does the sensation have shape, volume, texture, color? How does it affect me to feel this? Is there anything difficult about feeling this? Is it familiar? How old do I feel when I feel this? What happens as I feel it directly?
- At this point, you might begin associating a sensation with a memory or a particular feeling like sadness or loneliness. And you might have a reaction, might want to close down, go away, stop writing. Remember that a sensa-

tion is an immediate, primary experience located in the body, whereas a reaction is a secondary experience located in the mind. Some examples of reactions are: the desire to eat compulsively, telling yourself that your pain will never end, comparing how or what you feel to how you want to feel, comparing the present experience to your past experience, comparing yourself to someone else, making up a story about what is going on.

When you notice that you are reacting to what you are experiencing, come back to your body. Sense what is going on in your chest, your legs, your back, your belly. Inquiry is about allowing your direct and immediate experience to unfold; it is not about a story you are constructing in your mind.

• Recognize, name and disengage from The Voice. If you feel small, collapsed or powerless, it is usually a sign that The Voice is present. The Voice says things like "You will never be good enough"; "You will never change"; "You deserve to suffer"; "You are a failure/a bad person/unlovable/stupid/worthless/fat/ugly." Any feelings of shame are a response to The Voice.

251

To continue with the inquiry, you must disengage from The Voice, since its intent is to keep you circumscribed by *its definition of safe and to maintain the status quo.*

If recognizing its presence does not dispel it, you can say, "Back off!" or "Go away!" or "Go pick on someone your own size." Keep it short. Keep it simple. A successful disengagement defuses The Voice and releases the sensations.

- Whenever you notice that you are engaged in a reaction or are distracted, confused, numb or out of touch, go back to sensing your body.
- Pay attention to secrets, thoughts or feelings you've censored. When those arise, be curious about them. Be curious about what's hidden in them.
- Don't try to direct the inquiry with your mind. If you have an agenda or preferences (i.e., you don't want to feel needy or angry or hateful), the inquiry won't unfold. As the Tibetan Buddhists say, "Be like a child, astonished at everything."

Remember: Inquiry is a practice. It's not something you "get" the first or tenth time around. You don't do inquiry to get something; you do it because you want to find out who you are when you are not conditioned by your past or your ideas of what a good person is supposed to be. Each time you do it, you learn more. Each time you learn more, you continue the process of dismantling the stale, repetitive version of your (ego) self. With each inquiry, you have the chance to discover that you are not who you think you are. What a relief.

# THE EATING GUIDELINES

1. Eat when you are hungry.
2. Eat sitting down in a calm environment. This does not include the car.
3. Eat without distractions. Distractions include radio, television, newspapers, books, intense or anxiety-producing conversations or music.
4. Eat what your body wants.
5. Eat until you are satisfied.
6. Eat (with the intention of being) in full view of others.
7. Eat with enjoyment, gusto and pleasure.

# ABOUT THE AUTHOR

**Geneen Roth** is the author of eight books, including the bestselling *When Food Is Love* and *The Craggy Hole in My Heart and the Cat Who Fixed It,* a memoir. She lives in Northern California with her husband. For more information about her work, please visit www.geneenroth.com and follow her on Twitter @WomenFoodGod.

The employees of Thorndike Press hope you have enjoyed this Large Print book. All our Thorndike, Wheeler, and Kennebec Large Print titles are designed for easy reading, and all our books are made to last. Other Thorndike Press Large Print books are available at your library, through selected bookstores, or directly from us.

For information about titles, please call:
(800) 223-1244

or visit our Web site at:
http://gale.cengage.com/thorndike

To share your comments, please write:
Publisher
Thorndike Press
295 Kennedy Memorial Drive
Waterville, ME 04901